MELISA'S TRAVEL GUIDES

France Travel Guide

An Essential Guide to a Memorable Trips Ever | Hidden Gems, Outdoor Adventures, Local Tips, Best Beaches... With Tips On Things To Do...etc

Copyright © 2023 by Melisa's Travel Guides

All rights reserved. No part of this publication may be reproduced, stored or transmitted in any form or by any means, electronic, mechanical, photocopying, recording, scanning, or otherwise without written permission from the publisher. It is illegal to copy this book, post it to a website, or distribute it by any other means without permission.

First edition

This book was professionally typeset on Reedsy.
Find out more at reedsy.com

Contents

Disclaimer		vi
How To Use This Guide		vii
Introduction		viii
	Welcome To France	viii
	Why Visit France?	ix
1	Planning Your Trip	1
	When To Visit	3
	Visa and Entry Requirements	5
	Budgeting and Costs for France	7
	Itinerary Suggestions	9
2	France at a Glance	12
	Geography and Regions	12
	History and Culture	14
	Language and Communication	16
	Currency and Banking	18
3	Getting Around	20
	Transportation Options	20
	Travel Tips	22
	Driving in France	25
4	Accommodation	29
	Hotels and Resorts Hotels	29
	Vacation Rentals	31
	Bed and Breakfasts	33
	Camping and Hostels	35
5	Must-Visit Destinations	38
	Paris	38

	Île-de-France	40
	Normandy	42
	Brittany	43
	The Loire Valley	45
	Dordogne	46
	Provence	48
	French Riviera	49
	The French Alps	51
6	Other Regions of France	54
	Burgundy	54
	Champagne	56
	Alsace	58
	Basque Country	60
	Corsica	62
7	Exploring French Cuisine	64
	French Culinary Traditions	64
	Iconic French Dishes	67
	Dining Etiquette	69
	Food and Wine Regions	71
8	Cultural Experiences	74
	Museums and Art Galleries	74
	Theaters and Performances	77
	Festivals and Events	79
	Historical Sites	82
9	Outdoor Adventures	85
	Hiking and Trekking	85
	Skiing and Winter Sports	87
	Beaches and Water Sports	89
	Cycling and Cycling Routes	92
10	Shopping in France	95
	Souvenirs and Gifts	95
	Local Markets	97
	High-End Shopping	99

	Antique Hunting	101
11	Language and Travel Tips	104
	Common Phrases	104
	Travel Safety	105
	Etiquette and Customs	107
	Packing Essentials	109
	Packing tips	111
12	Conclusion	113
	Further Reading and Resources	113
	Feedback and Contact Information	115
Final Note		118

Disclaimer

There are no photographs in this trip guide. Because I am unable to offer photographs for all of the places and activities described in the book, this is the case.

Please accept my apologies for any inconveniences this may cause. I hope you still find this information useful as you plan your trip to France.

How To Use This Guide

This guide is meant to help you learn more about France, from its culture and history to its food and language. It is split into several parts, each of which covers a different topic.

To use this book, simply start at the beginning and read through each part. You can also skip around to different parts if you are interested in a particular topic.

Here are some helpful tips for using this guide:

- Read the table of contents: The table of contents will give you a good idea of the topics covered in the book.
- Use the index: The index is a list of all the topics covered in the book. You can use it to find specific information quickly and easily.
- Skim the text: Before you read a part in detail, skim it first to get the main idea. This will help you to understand the part better when you read it more carefully.
- Take notes: As you read, take notes on the information that you find most important. This will help you to remember the information and to come back to it later.
- Discuss what you learn: Talk to your friends, family, or teachers about what you learn from this book. This will help you to understand the knowledge better and to keep it longer.

Introduction

Welcome To France

France is a country of unmatched beauty and charm, with a rich history and culture that goes back ages. From the busy streets of Paris to the rolling fields of Burgundy, France has something to offer everyone.

Whether you're interested in art, building, food, wine, or simply want to experience the French way of life, you're sure to find what you're looking for in France.

Here are just a few of the things that make France such a wonderful place:

Iconic buildings: France is home to some of the most famous landmarks in the world, including the Eiffel Tower, the Louvre Museum, and the Palace of Versailles.

World-class cuisine: French cuisine is renowned for its elegance and sophistication. From Michelin-starred places to cozy bars, there's something to please every palate.

Stunning scenery: France is blessed with a diverse landscape, from the snow-capped Alps to the sun-drenched ports of the Riviera.

Vibrant culture: France has a rich cultural history, which is obvious in its art, music, writing, and theater.

Charming towns and villages: France is dotted with charming towns and villages, each with its own unique character.

No matter what your hobbies are, you're sure to have a great holiday in France.

Why Visit France?

There are many reasons to visit France, but here are just a few of the most compelling:

Iconic sites: France is home to some of the most iconic landmarks in the world, including the Eiffel Tower, the Louvre Museum, and the Palace of Versailles. These sites are a must-see for any guest to France.

World-class cuisine: French cuisine is renowned for its elegance and sophistication. From Michelin-starred places to cozy bars, there's something to please every palate. France is also home to some of the world's best wines, so be sure to try a few while you're there.

Stunning scenery: France is blessed with a diverse landscape, from the snow-capped Alps to the sun-drenched ports of the Riviera. Whether you're looking for a relaxing beach trip or an exciting mountain break, you're sure to find it in France.

Vibrant culture: France has a rich cultural history, which is obvious in its art, music, writing, and theater. There's always something going in France, so be sure to check the local calendar to see what events are taking place during your visit.

Charming towns and villages: France is dotted with charming towns and villages, each with its own unique character. Whether you're interested in history, culture, or simply want to experience the French way of life, be sure to visit a few of these charming towns during your trip.

In addition to these general reasons, there are also many special reasons to visit France, based on your hobbies. For example, if you're interested in art, you might want to visit the Louvre Museum, the Musée d'Orsay, and the Centre Pompidou. If you're interested in history, you might want to visit the Palace of Versailles, the Château de Chambord, and the D-Day beaches in Normandy. And if you're interested in food and wine, you might want to visit the wineries of Bordeaux and Burgundy, or the markets of Provence.

No matter what your interests are, you're sure to find something to love in France. It's a truly beautiful country with something to offer everyone.

Here are a few more specific reasons to visit France:

- **To experience the French way of life:** France is known for its relaxed pace of life and its focus on enjoying the good things in life. From leisurely meals at sidewalk cafes to leisurely strolls through beautiful towns, France is the perfect place to relax and recover.
- **To learn about French culture:** France has a rich and lively culture that is obvious in its art, architecture, food, and music. A visit to France is a great chance to learn more about this interesting country and to experience it directly.
- **To improve your French skills:** If you're learning French, a visit to France is the best way to practice your skills in a real-world setting. Immerse yourself in the language and society by speaking French with locals and viewing French-language sites.
- **To make lasting memories:** France is a truly special place that will leave you with lasting memories. From the amazing scenery to the delicious food to the lovely people, France is a place that will stay with you long

after you leave.

1

Planning Your Trip

Planning a trip to France can be stressful, but it doesn't have to be. Here are a few tips to help you get started:

1. Choose when to visit: France is a beautiful place to visit year-round, but each season has its own special charms. Spring and fall are ideal for mild weather and smaller people, while summer is the best time to enjoy the outdoors. Winter is a great time to visit the French Alps for skiing and snowboarding.

2. Decide on your budget: France can be an expensive place to visit, but there are ways to save money. For example, you can stay in hostels or guesthouses instead of hotels, eat at budget-friendly places, and take advantage of free activities, such as viewing parks and museums.

3. Book your flights and accommodation: Flights and lodging tend to be more expensive during peak season, so it's important to book them in advance, especially if you're going on a budget. There are a variety of websites where you can book trips and lodgings, such as Kayak, Expedia, and Airbnb.

4. Plan your transportation: France has a well-developed transportation system, making it easy to get around the country by train, bus, or car. If you're planning on hiring a car, be sure to book one in advance and prepare yourself with the French driving rules.

5. Learn a few simple French phrases: Knowing a few simple French words will make your trip more fun and easier to navigate. Here are a few important phrases:

```
Bonjour (hello)
Bonne journée (have a good day)
Merci (thank you)
S'il vous plaît (please)
Au revoir (goodbye)
```

6. Research your destinations: France has a lot to offer guests, so it's important to decide which areas and places you want to visit. If you're first-time guests, you might want to focus on Paris and the nearby Île-de-France area. Other famous places include the Loire Valley, the French Riviera, and the French Alps.

7. Create a packing list: Be sure to pack everything you need for your trip, including clothes for all types of weather, comfy shoes, and a power charger.

Here are a few extra tips for planning your trip to France:

- **Purchase travel insurance:** Travel insurance can protect you in the event of unexpected events, such as lost bags, flight cancellations, or medical problems.
- **Apply for a visa (if needed):** Citizens of most countries do not need a visa to visit France for up to 90 days. However, it's always a good idea to check the visa rules before you journey.
- **Get vaccinated:** It's a good idea to make sure that you are up-to-date on all of your shots before you travel to France.
- **Be aware of your surroundings:** France is a generally safe country, but

it's important to be aware of your surroundings and to take steps against small theft.

By following these tips, you can plan a great and enjoyable trip to France.

When To Visit

France is a beautiful place to visit year-round, but each season has its own special charms. Here is a more thorough look at the best time to visit France, based on your interests:

Spring (April to June): Spring is a great time to visit France for nice weather and fewer people. The flowers are in bloom, and the scenery is lush and green. This is a good time to visit Paris, the Loire Valley, and the French Riviera.

Summer (July to August): Summer is the peak tourist season in France, so expect bigger crowds and higher prices. However, the weather is warm and sunny, making it ideal for outdoor activities, such as swimming, hikes, and biking. This is a good time to visit the French Alps and the beaches of the French Riviera.

Fall (September to October): Fall is a shoulder season in France, so you can enjoy mild weather and smaller groups. The leaves are changing color, and the scenery is beautiful. This is a good time to visit Paris, the Loire Valley, and the French countryside.

Winter (November to March): Winter is the off-season in France, so you can enjoy the best deals on flights and accommodation. However, the weather can be cold and snowy, so be sure to pack properly. This is a good time to visit the French Alps for skiing and snowboarding.

Here is a more thorough look at the pros and cons of visiting France during each season:

Spring:

Pros: Mild weather, fewer crowds, flowers in bloom, green countryside

Cons: Some sites may be closed for renovation

Summer:

Pros: Warm weather, sunny days, great for outdoor activities

Cons: Large crowds, high prices, some sites may be closed due to heat

Fall:

Pros: Mild weather, smaller crowds, beautiful fall foliage

Cons: Some sites may be closed for the off-season

Winter:

Pros: Best deals on flights and lodging, great for skiing and snowboarding

Cons: Cold weather, snowy conditions, some sites may be closed due to snow

Ultimately, the best time to visit France relies on your individual interests. If you're looking for warm weather and fewer people, spring and fall are good choices. If you're looking for warm weather and sunny days, summer is a good choice. And if you're looking for the best deals on flights and lodgings, winter is a good choice.

Visa and Entry Requirements

Visa Requirements

Citizens of most countries can visit France for up to 90 days without a visa. However, there are a few exceptions, so it's always a good idea to check the visa rules before you journey. You can find more information on the website of the French Ministry of Foreign Affairs.

Entry Requirements

All guests to France must have a legal visa that is good for at least three months after the planned date of departure. You may also be asked to show proof of return journey and sufficient funds for your stay.

Additional Requirements for Minors

Minors going to France without a parent or legal guardian must have written permission from at least one parent or legal guardian.

Visa Application Process

If you do need a visa to visit France, you can apply at a French office or consulate in your home country. The visa application process can take several weeks, so it's important to start planning your trip early.

Required Documents for Visa Application

The needed papers for a visa application change based on the type of visa you are asking for. However, some common necessary papers include:

- A finished visa application form
- A current passport
- Two passport-size photos
- Proof of return travel
- Proof of sufficient funds for your stay
- Medical insurance
- A letter of welcome (if needed)

Visa Fees

The visa fee for a France visa also changes based on the type of visa you are asking for. However, most vacation passes cost around 80 euros.

Tips for Applying for a France Visa

Here are a few tips for asking for a France visa:

- Make sure to start planning your trip early and apply for your visa at least several weeks in advance.
- Gather all of the needed papers before you start the application process.
- Fill out the visa application form carefully and correctly.
- Submit all of the necessary papers and pay the visa fee.
- Be prepared to answer questions about your trip during your visa interview.

Entry Procedures at the French Border

When you arrive at the French border, you will be asked to show your passport and other travel papers. You may also be asked to show proof of return journey and sufficient funds for your stay.

If you are a citizen of a country that is not free from visa rules, you will need to show your visa to the border guard.

The visa and entry conditions for France are pretty simple. However, it's always a good idea to check the standards before you journey and to start planning your trip early.

Budgeting and Costs for France

France is a beautiful place, but it can also be an expensive one. However, there are ways to pay for a trip to France without losing quality. Here are a few tips:

Accommodation

Accommodation is one of the biggest costs on any trip, but it doesn't have to be. There are a number of budget-friendly housing choices in France, such as hotels, guesthouses, and Airbnb rentals.

If you're going with a group, you can save money by staying in a hotel or Airbnb rental. Hostels usually charge around €20-30 per night, while Airbnb rentals start at around €50 per night.

If you're going solo, you can save money by staying in a guesthouse or cheap hotel. Guesthouses usually charge around €40-50 per night, while cheap hotels start at around €60 per night.

Food and Drink

Food and drink can also be an expensive cost in France. However, there are ways to save money without losing quality.

One way to save money on food is to eat at smaller, local places instead of tourist traps. Local places generally charge less than tourist traps, and they often give better food quality.

Another way to save money on food is to cook your own meals. If you're living in a hostel or Airbnb rental with a kitchen, you can save a lot of money by cooking your own meals.

Transportation

Transportation is another cost to keep in mind when planning for a trip to France. However, there are ways to save money on transportation without losing ease.

One way to save money on transportation is to use public transportation. Public transportation in France is quick and cheap. You can purchase a single ticket for €1.90, or you can buy a day pass for €5.30.

Another way to save money on transportation is to rent a bicycle. Bicycles are a great way to get around Paris and other French cities. You can rent a bicycle for around €10 per day.

Activities

There are many free and low-cost activities to enjoy in France. Here are a few ideas:

- Visit museums and art galleries. Many museums and art galleries in France offer free admission on certain days of the week.
- Take a walk through a park or garden. There are many beautiful parks and gardens in France that are free to enter.
- Visit a local market. Markets are a great way to experience French culture and to find fresh, local produce.

- Attend a free event. There are often free concerts, festivals, and other events happening in France.

It's possible to budget for a trip to France without sacrificing quality. By following the tips above, you can save money on accommodation, food and drink, transportation, and activities.

Here is a sample budget for a week-long trip to Paris for a solo traveler:

```
Accommodation: €300-400
Food and drink: €200-300 Transportation: €50-100
Activities: €50-100
Total: €600-800
```

This is just a sample budget, and your actual expenses may vary depending on your travel style and preferences. However, this budget should give you a good starting point for planning your trip.

Itinerary Suggestions

Here are a few itinerary suggestions for a trip to France:

Paris:

Day 1: Arrive in Paris and check into your hotel. Take a walk around the city center and visit the Eiffel Tower, the Louvre Museum, and the Notre Dame Cathedral.

Day 2: Visit the Palace of Versailles, a UNESCO World Heritage Site.

Day 3: Visit the Musée d'Orsay, a museum housed in a former railway station with a collection of Impressionist and Post-Impressionist art.

Day 4: Take a boat cruise on the Seine River and visit the Musée Rodin, a museum dedicated to the work of sculptor Auguste Rodin.

Day 5: Visit the Musée Picasso, a museum dedicated to the work of artist Pablo Picasso.

Loire Valley:

Day 1: Arrive in the Loire Valley and check into your hotel. Visit the Château de Chambord, one of the most famous castles in the world.

Day 2: Visit the Château de Chenonceau, a castle that spans the Cher River.

Day 3: Visit the Château de Villandry, a castle with beautiful gardens.

Day 4: Visit the city of Tours, the capital of the Loire Valley.

Day 5: Depart from the Loire Valley.

French Riviera:

Day 1: Arrive in Nice and check into your hotel. Visit the Promenade des Anglais, a seaside promenade with stunning views of the Mediterranean Sea.

Day 2: Visit the city of Cannes, home to the Cannes Film Festival.

Day 3: Visit the city of Saint-Tropez, a popular tourist destination with beautiful beaches and a lively nightlife.

Day 4: Visit the city of Èze, a medieval village perched on a hilltop.

Day 5: Depart from the French Riviera.

These are just a few itinerary suggestions, and you can customize them to fit your interests and budget. For example, if you're interested in history, you could spend more time visiting castles and historical sites. If you're interested in art, you could spend more time visiting museums. And if you're on a tight budget, you could focus on free and low-cost activities.

No matter what your interests are, you're sure to have a wonderful time in France. It's a beautiful country with something to offer everyone.

2

France at a Glance

Geography and Regions

France is situated in Western Europe, surrounded by the Atlantic Ocean to the west, the English Channel to the north, the North Sea to the northeast, Belgium, Luxembourg, and Germany to the east, Switzerland, Italy, and Monaco to the south, and Spain and Andorra to the southwest. It has a total size of 640,679 square kilometers (247,368 sq mi), making it the largest country in Western Europe.

France is split into 18 governmental regions, which are further separated into 96 departments. The regions are:

- Auvergne-Rhône-Alpes
- Bourgogne-Franche-Comté
- Brittany
- Centre-Val de Loire
- Corsica
- Grand Est
- Hauts-de-France

- Île-de-France
- Normandy
- Nouvelle-Aquitaine
- Occitanie
- Pays de la Loire
- Provence-Alpes-Côte d'Azur

France has a varied landscape, with mountains, fields, and woods. The Alps and the Pyrenees are the two major mountain ranges in France. The Alps are located in the southeastern corner of the country, while the Pyrenees are located in the southwestern corner of the country.

The Paris Basin is a big area that covers much of northern and central France. The Loire Valley is another big area that is found in the west-central part of the country.

France is also home to a number of forests, including the Vosges Forest, the Ardennes Forest, and the Landes Forest.

Major Cities

The biggest city in France is Paris, the capital. Other major towns include Marseille, Lyon, Toulouse, Nice, and Nantes.

Climate

France has a moderate climate, with mild winters and warm summers. However, the temperature changes based on the area. The north of France has a more marine climate, while the south of France has a more Mediterranean climate.

Natural Resources

France is rich in natural materials, including coal, iron ore, bauxite, and uranium. It is also a big source of farm goods, such as wheat, corn, and grapes.

Economy

France is a big economic power, with the sixth-largest economy in the world. The French economy is built on a range of businesses, including industry, agriculture, and tourism.

France is a beautiful and diverse country with something to offer everyone. From its beautiful scenery to its rich history and culture, France is a country that is sure to leave a lasting impression.

History and Culture

France has a rich and complicated past, going back to the Stone Age. The first known settlers of France were the Neanderthals, who arrived in the region around 400,000 years ago. The Neanderthals were finally replaced by the Cro-Magnons, who arrived in the region around 40,000 years ago.

The first known culture in France was the Gauls, who arrived in the area around 2000 BC. The Gauls were a Celtic people who were split into a number of groups. The Gauls were known for their fierce fighters and their rich culture.

In 58 BC, the Roman Empire captured Gaul. The Romans ruled Gaul for over 400 years, and during that time, they brought Roman law, language, and culture to the area.

In the 5th century AD, the Roman Empire fell, and Gaul was attacked by a number of Germanic groups. The Franks, one of the Germanic groups, finally won control of Gaul, and in 800 AD, Charlemagne, the King of the Franks, was named Holy Roman Emperor.

The Holy Roman Empire fell in the 15th century, and France emerged as a unified country. France became a major power in Europe during the Renaissance, and it played a key part in the Age of Enlightenment.

In 1789, the French Revolution began. The French Revolution was a time of extreme social and political change in France that had a major effect on France and the rest of the world. The French Revolution led to the end of the monarchy and the creation of the First French Republic.

In 1804, Napoleon Bonaparte crowned himself Emperor of France. Napoleon led France to success in a number of wars, and he expanded the French Empire to include much of Europe. However, Napoleon was finally beaten in the Battle of Waterloo in 1815.

After Napoleon's loss, France entered a time of relative peace and security. The French economy grew during this time, and France became a major culture center.

In the 20th century, France was involved in two world wars. France was beaten by Germany in World War II, but it was freed by the Allies in 1944.

After World War II, France was a founding member of the United Nations and the North Atlantic Treaty Organization (NATO). France has played a major part in the European Union, and it is one of the most wealthy countries in the world.

French Culture

French culture is a varied and lively culture that has been affected by a number of factors, including the country's rich past, its physical position, and its people.

France is known for its art, music, writing, and food. French artists such as Claude Monet, Vincent van Gogh, and Auguste Rodin have made some of the most famous works of art in the world. French artists such as Edith Piaf, Charles Aznavour, and Daft Punk have created some of the most famous songs in the world. French writers such as Victor Hugo, Émile Zola, and Albert Camus have created some of the most important works of writing in the world. French food is famous for its grace and beauty.

France is also known for its fashion sense. Paris is one of the world's top fashion centers, and French fashion designers such as Coco Chanel and Christian Dior have made some of the most famous fashion designs in the world.

France has a rich and complicated past and society. The country is home to some of the world's most famous art, music, writing, food, and fashion. France is a truly unique and special country, and it is a country that is sure to leave a lasting impact on tourists.

Language and Communication

France is a multilingual country, with French being the official language. However, there are a number of other regional languages spoken in France, such as Breton, Corsican, Occitan, and Basque.

French is a Romance language, and it is one of the most widely spoken languages in the world. French is spoken by over 270 million people globally, and it is the official language of 29 countries.

French is a highly complicated language, but it is also a very beautiful language.

French is known for its beautiful language and its rich words.

French Communication

The French are known for their serious and polite conversation style. French people usually use names when greeting others, such as Monsieur (Mr.), Madame (Ms.), and Mademoiselle (Miss). French people also usually use the vous form of address when speaking to someone they do not know well. The vous form of address is more official than the tu form of address, which is usually used when speaking to friends and family.

The French also place a high value on non-verbal communication. French people use movements and facial emotions heavily when speaking. For example, a French person might shrug their shoulders to indicate boredom or a French person might raise their eyes to indicate surprise.

French language and conversation are complicated and subtle, but they are also important for understanding French society. By learning a few simple French words and knowing the French conversation style, you can have a more enjoyable and satisfying experience when visiting France.

Here are a few simple French words that you may find useful:

```
Bonjour (hello)
Bonne journée (have a good day)
Merci (thank you)
S'il vous plaît (please)
Au revoir (goodbye)
Excusez-moi (excuse me)
Oui (yes)
Non (no)
Je comprends (I understand)
Je ne comprends pas (I don't understand)
```

Parlez-vous anglais? (Do you speak English?)

Currency and Banking

The official currency of France is the euro (€). The euro is also the official currency of 19 other countries in the European Union.

Euros come in both coins and bills. The coins are offered in amounts of 1, 2, 5, 10, 20, and 50 cents and €1 and €2. The banknotes are offered in amounts of €5, €10, €20, €50, €100, €200, and €500.

Banking in France

France has a well-developed banking system. There are a number of big French banks, such as BNP Paribas, Crédit Agricole, and Société Générale. There are also a number of foreign banks that operate in France.

Most French banks offer a wide range of services, including cash and savings accounts, credit cards, loans, and investment services.

Using Credit Cards in France

Credit cards are widely accepted in France. Most companies in France accept Visa, Mastercard, and American Express. However, it is always a good idea to check with the business to see if they accept your credit card before you make a purchase.

Using ATMs in France

ATMs are widely found in France. You can find ATMs in banks, post offices, and other public places.

To use an ATM in France, you will need to put your credit or debit card and enter your PIN. You will then be able to receive cash in euros.

Exchange Rates

The exchange rate between the euro and other currencies changes daily. You can check the current exchange rate on a website such as XE.com.

Tips for Managing Your Money in France

Here are a few tips for handling your money in France:

- Budget for your trip before you go: This will help you to track your spending and to avoid overspending.
- Exchange your cash for euros before you go: This will save you time and money.
- Use credit cards sparingly: Credit cards can charge high interest rates, so it is important to use them carefully.
- Be aware of changing rates: Exchange rates vary daily, so it is important to be aware of the current exchange rate before you switch your cash.
- Keep track of your spending: This will help you to stay on budget and to avoid overspending.

3

Getting Around

Transportation Options

France has a well-developed transportation system, making it easy to get around the country by train, bus, car, or plane.

Trains

Trains are one of the most popular ways to get around France. The French national railway company, SNCF, runs a network of high-speed trains (TGVs) and regional trains. TGV trains can hit speeds of up to 320 km/h, making them a fast and easy way to travel between big towns. Regional trains are slower than TGV trains, but they serve smaller towns and villages.

Buses

Buses are another cheap way to get around France. There are a number of bus companies that run interstate and regional bus routes. Intercity buses can be a good option for traveling between big cities, while regional buses can be a good option for traveling to smaller towns and villages.

Cars

Renting a car is a good choice for tourists who want to have the freedom to explore France at their own pace. However, it is important to remember that driving in France can be difficult, especially in big towns. French drivers are known for being rude and for not following the rules of the road.

Planes

Air travel is a good choice for tourists who need to move big places quickly. There are a number of local companies that run flights between major French towns. There are also a number of foreign companies that run trips to and from France.

Other Transportation Options

In addition to the mobility methods mentioned above, there are a number of other ways to get around France, including:

Ferries: Ferries run between France and a number of other countries, including the United Kingdom, Ireland, and Spain. Ferries can also be used to journey between the center of France and the islands of Corsica and Sardinia.

Taxis: Taxis are available in all big French towns. Taxis can be a quick way to get around, but they can also be expensive.

Ride-hailing apps: Ride-hailing apps such as Uber and Lyft are available in some French cities. Ride-hailing apps can be a more cheap way to get around than cars.

Bicycles: Bicycles can be a good way to get around smaller towns and villages. There are a number of bicycle hire companies that run in France.

Public transportation: Public transportation is offered in all big French towns. Public transportation systems usually include buses, metros, and trams. Public transportation is a pretty cheap way to get around.

Tips for Choosing the Best Transportation Option

The best transportation choice for you will rely on your income, your trip schedule, and your personal tastes. If you are on a tight budget, buses are a good choice. If you need to move big places fast, air travel is a good choice. If you want to have the freedom to explore France at your own pace, getting a car is a good choice.

No matter which transportation option you choose, be sure to study your choices in advance and to book your tickets ahead of time, especially if you are going during busy season.

Travel Tips

Here are some travel tips for your trip to France:

> **Before you go:**

- Book your flights and accommodation in advance,especially if you're going during peak season (June-August).
- Purchase travel insurance to protect yourself against unexpected events, such as illness, lost bags, or flight cancelation.
- Learn a few basic French phrases: This will help you to talk with people and to get around more quickly.
- Exchange your currency for euros before you go. This will save you time and money.

- Pack light to avoid paying travel fees.

When you arrive:

- Validate your transportation ticket before you take the train, bus, or metro.
- Be aware of pickpockets in crowded areas, such as train stops and tourist sites.
- Don't be afraid to ask for help if you're lost or need assistance. Most French people are happy to help tourists.

Things to do:

Visit the Eiffel Tower: The Eiffel Tower is the most famous feature in Paris and one of the most popular tourist sites in the world.

Explore the Louvre Museum: The Louvre Museum is one of the biggest and most famous museums in the world. It is home to a vast collection of art and artifacts, including the Mona Lisa and the Venus de Milo.

Take a walk through the Tuileries Gardens: The Tuileries Gardens are a beautiful public park located next to the Louvre Museum. They are a great place to relax and people-watch.

Visit the Notre Dame Cathedral: The Notre Dame Cathedral is a Gothic cathedral situated on the Île de la Cité in Paris. It is one of the most famous tourist sites in Paris.

Take a boat tour on the Seine River: A boat tour on the Seine River is a great way to see some of the most famous sites in Paris, such as the Eiffel Tower, the Louvre Museum, and the Notre Dame Cathedral.

Visit the Palace of Versailles: The Palace of Versailles is a former royal palace situated in Versailles, France. It is one of the most famous tourist sites in France.

Explore the French Riviera: The French Riviera is a coastal area in southeastern France. It is known for its beautiful beaches, lovely towns, and glitzy nightlife.

Visit the Loire Valley: The Loire Valley is a place in central France. It is known for its beautiful scenery, its buildings, and its wine.

Sample the French cuisine: France is known for its world-class food. Be sure to try some of the local foods, such as escargots, foie gras, and coq au vin.

Tips for saving money:

- Eat at local restaurants: Local restaurants are typically less expensive than tourist traps.
- Avoid eating at restaurants in tourist areas: Restaurants in tourist areas are typically more expensive than restaurants in other areas of the city.
- Take advantage of free activities: There are many free activities to enjoy in France, such as visiting parks, museums, and churches.
- Purchase a travel pass: A travel pass can save you money on transportation costs.
- Walk or bike whenever possible: Walking and biking are great ways to get around France and to save money on transportation costs.

France is a beautiful country with something to offer everyone.

Driving in France

Driving in France can be a great way to see the country and discover its many secret gems. However, it is important to be aware of the different driving rules and laws in France before you hit the road.

Driving Requirements

To drive in France, you must be at least 18 years old and hold a legal driver's license. You may also need to carry an International Driving Permit (IDP), but this is not needed if you have a driver's license from an EU country or a country that has signed the Geneva Convention on Road Traffic.

Driving Rules and Regulations

Here are some of the most important driving rules and laws in France:

- Drive on the right-hand side of the road.
- Use a hands-free device if you need to use your phone while driving.
- Wear a seatbelt at all times.
- Children under the age of 10 must ride in a kid seat.
- The speed limit on freeways is 130 km/h (81 mph), on national roads it is 90 km/h (56 mph), and in urban areas it is 50 km/h (31 mph).
- Be aware of the different road signs and marks in France.

Tips for Driving in France

- Here are some tips for driving in France:
- **Be aware of pushy cars:** French drivers are known for being rude and for not following the rules of the road.

- **Be careful when driving in small streets and towns:** Many streets and towns in France are small and curvy, so it is important to be careful when driving.
- **Be aware of the different types of roads in France:** There are a number of different types of roads in France, including motorways, national roads, and regional roads. It is important to be aware of the different types of roads when planning your trip.
- **Be aware of the different types of tolls in France:** There are a number of different kinds of tolls in France, including tolls on roads and tolls on certain bridges and tunnels. It is important to be aware of the different types of tolls when planning your journey.

Emergencies

If you have a problem while driving in France, you can call 112 for help. This is the emergency number for all types of situations in France, including police, fire, and medical.

Driving in France can be a great way to see the country and discover its many secret gems. However, it is important to be aware of the different driving rules and laws in France before you hit the road.

Public Transportation

Public transportation in France is fast, cheap, and approachable. It is a great way to get around the country, whether you are visiting big cities or discovering smaller towns and villages.

Types of Public Transportation

France has a range of public transportation choices, including:

Metro: The metro is a fast transit system that runs in big towns such as Paris, Lyon, and Marseille. It is a fast and handy way to get around the city.

Bus: Buses are available in all big cities and towns in France. They are a relatively cheap way to get around, but they can be slow in traffic.

Tram: Trams are found in some big cities and towns in France. They are a fast and handy way to get around, and they often offer beautiful views of the city.

Train: Trains are a great way to get around France, especially for longer routes. The French national railway company, SNCF, runs a network of high-speed trains (TGVs) and regional trains. TGV trains can hit speeds of up to 320 km/h, making them a fast and easy way to travel between big towns. Regional trains are slower than TGV trains, but they serve smaller towns and village.

How to Use Public Transportation

Public transportation in France is easy to use. To use the metro, bus, or train, you will need to buy a ticket. Tickets can be bought at machines placed in stops or on board cars.

To use the train, you will need to buy a ticket at a train stop. Tickets can be bought in advance online or at the station.

Tips for Using Public Transportation

Here are a few tips for using public transportation in France:

- Validate your ticket before you take the train, bus, or metro.
- Be aware of pickpockets in busy places, such as train stops and tourist sites.
- Don't be afraid to ask for help if you're lost or need assistance. Most French people are happy to help tourists.

Public transportation in France is a great way to get around the country. It is quick, cheap, and available. By following the tips above, you can have a safe and enjoyable time using public transportation in France.

4

Accommodation

Hotels and Resorts Hotels

France has a wide range of hotels to choose from, based on your price and tastes. You can find expensive hotels in big cities like Paris and Nice, as well as budget-friendly hotels in smaller towns and villages.

Here are a few of the most famous hotels in France:

Hôtel Plaza Athénée: This upscale hotel is located in the heart of Paris, and it has been home to celebrities and royalty for decades.

Hôtel de Crillon: This historic hotel is also located in the heart of Paris, and it is known for its beautiful rooms and excellent service.

Four Seasons Hotel George V, Paris: This Four Seasons hotel is situated in the Champs-Élysées area of Paris, and it offers beautiful views of the Eiffel Tower.

La Réserve Paris Hotel and gym: This five-star hotel is located on the Avenue

Gabriel, and it offers luxury rooms and a world-class gym.

Hotel de Russie: This boutique hotel is situated in the Saint-Germain-des-Prés area of Paris, and it is known for its stylish rooms and its busy bar and restaurant.

If you are looking for a more budget-friendly choice, there are also a number of cheap hotels in France. Here are a few of the most popular budget-friendly hotels in France:

Hotel Metropol: This two-star hotel is located in the Latin Quarter of Paris, and it offers clean and cozy rooms at a reasonable price.

Generator Hostel Paris Nation: This hostel is located in the Nation area of Paris, and it offers a range of group rooms and private rooms at a budget-friendly price.

Hotel des Arts Montmartre: This three-star hotel is located in the Montmartre area of Paris, and it offers charming rooms and stunning views of the city.

Hotel Metropol Nice: This two-star hotel is located in the heart of Nice, and it offers clean and cozy rooms at a reasonable price

Hostel Vertigo Vieux Lyon: This hotel is situated in the Vieux Lyon area of Lyon, and it offers a range of group rooms and private rooms at a budget-friendly price.

Resorts France is also home to a number of world-class resorts. Here are a few of the most famous spots in France:

La Villa Madie: This five-star resort is located in the town of Cassis, and it offers luxury rooms, a world-class gym, and stunning views of the Mediterranean Sea.

Hôtel du Cap-Eden-Roc: This five-star resort is located in the town of Cap d'Antibes, and it has been a favorite of celebrities and royalty for decades.

Terre Blanche Hotel Spa Golf Resort: This five-star resort is situated in the town of Tourrettes-sur-Loup, and it offers luxury rooms, a world-class hotel, and two championship golf courses.

Royal Barrière: This five-star resort is located on the beachfront in La Baule, and it offers luxury rooms, a world-class gym, and stunning views of the Atlantic Ocean.

Domaine des Etangs: This four-star resort is situated in the town of Massignac, and it offers a range of activities, including fishing, hiking, and biking.

No matter what your income or tastes are, you are sure to find the right hotel or resort in France.

Vacation Rentals

France is a beautiful country with a lot to offer tourists, from its stunning scenery to its rich past and culture. Vacation homes are a great way to experience France, as they offer the freedom to travel at your own pace and stay in unique and original places.

Here are a few of the most common types of vacation homes in France:

Gites: Gites are country houses that are usually found in small towns and rural places. They are a great choice for tourists who want to explore the French countryside.

Chateaux: Chateaux are houses that have been turned into luxury vacation homes. They are a great choice for tourists who want to experience the grandeur of French society.

Apartments: Apartments are a great choice for tourists who want to stay in the heart of a city or town. They are usually more cheap than hotels and offer more room and services.

Houses: Houses are a great choice for tourists who are going with a group or who want to have more room and privacy. They are typically found in neighborhood areas and offer a variety of features, such as swimming pools, parks, and parking.

Here are a few tips for picking a holiday rental in France:

- **Consider your budget:** Vacation homes can range in price from budget-friendly to luxury. It is important to set a price before you start your search so that you can find a rental that fits your needs.
- **Think about the location:** Do you want to stay in a city, town, or country area? Consider what you want to do during your trip and choose a rental that is located near the sites that you want to see.
- **Consider the perks:** What features are important to you? Some homes give features such as swimming pools, parks, parking, and Wi-Fi. Make sure to choose a rental that has the features that you need.
- **Read the reviews:** Before you book a rental, read reviews from other guests. This can help you to get an idea of the quality of the rental and the experience of other guests.

Once you have chosen a holiday rental, be sure to book it in advance, especially if you are going during busy season. You should also buy trip insurance to protect yourself against unexpected events.

Here are a few of the most famous vacation rental websites:

- Airbnb
- Vrbo
- HomeAway
- Booking.com
- Expedi

With so many different types of vacation rentals to choose from, you are sure to find the right rental for your holiday in France.

Bed and Breakfasts

Bed and breakfasts (B&Bs) are a great choice for tourists who want to experience France in a more real way. B&Bs are usually small, family-owned businesses that offer guests a chance to stay in a home and experience French culture directly.

Here are a few of the perks of staying in a B&B in France:

Authentic experience: B&Bs offer guests a chance to experience French culture directly. Guests can learn about French customs and traditions from their hosts, and they can also enjoy home-cooked meals made with fresh, local products.

More personal service: B&B hosts are usually more personal and responsive than hotel staff. They are happy to help guests with everything from planning their schedule to finding the best places.

More affordable: B&Bs are usually more cheap than hotels, especially if you are going with a group.

More flexibility: B&Bs offer guests more flexibility than hotels. Guests can usually check in and out at their comfort, and they can also come and go as they please.

If you are considering staying in a B&B in France, here are a few tips:

- **Book in advance:** B&Bs are often popular, especially during peak season. It is important to book your stay in advance, especially if you are going during the summer months.
- **Read reviews:** Before you book a B&B, read reviews from other guests. This can help you to get an idea of the quality of the B&B and the experience of other guests.
- **Ask about breakfast:** Some B&Bs offer a full breakfast, while others offer a simple breakfast. Be sure to ask about the food choices before you book your stay.
- **Be prepared to connect with your hosts:** B&B hosts are usually very nice and welcome. Be prepared to connect with your friends and learn about their society.

Here are a few of the most famous B&Bs in France:

La Maison Bleue: This B&B is located in the heart of Paris and offers guests a chance to stay in a charming Parisian flat.

Le B&B des Anges: This B&B is located in the Loire Valley and offers guests a chance to stay in a traditional French home.

Le Mas de la Bastide: This B&B is located in Provence and offers guests a chance to stay in a luxurious house with stunning views of the countryside.

ACCOMMODATION

La house Mimosa: This B&B is located in the French Riviera and offers guests a chance to stay in a stylish house with private beach access.

La Petite Auberge: This B&B is located in the Pyrenees and offers guests a chance to stay in a beautiful mountain house.

With so many great B&Bs to choose from, you are sure to find the right one for your holiday in France.

Camping and Hostels

Camping and hostelling are two great ways to travel on a budget and explore new cultures. Both choices offer a unique way to meet other tourists and connect with nature.

Camping

Camping is a great way to experience the outdoors and enjoy the natural beauty of France. There are many different types of campsites offered in France, from basic campgrounds with basic services to luxury campgrounds with all the bells and whistles.

When picking a spot, be sure to consider the following factors:

Location: Do you want to camp in a country area, near a town or city, or on the beach?

Amenities: What amenities are important to you? Some parks offer facilities such as swimming pools, bars, and gyms.

Price: Campsites can range in price from budget-friendly to luxury. Set a budget before you start your search so that you can find a spot that fits your needs.

Here are a few tips for camping in France:

- **Book in advance:** Campsites can fill up quickly, especially during peak season. It is important to book your spot in advance, especially if you are going during the summer months.
- **Be prepared for the weather:** The weather in France can change based on the area and the time of year. Be sure to pack for all types of weather, including rain, sun, and wind.
- **Bring your own gear:** You will need to bring your own camping gear, such as a tent, sleeping bag, and food tools. You can rent camping gear from some campgrounds, but it is generally cheaper to bring your own.
- **Leave no trace:** Be sure to leave your spot as you found it. Pack out all of your trash and dispose of it properly.

Hostels

Hostels are a great way to meet other tourists and save money on lodging. Hostels usually offer group rooms and private rooms at a budget-friendly price.

When picking a hotel, be sure to consider the following factors:

Spot: Do you want to stay in a hotel in a central spot or in a quieter neighborhood?

Amenities: What amenities are important to you? Some dorms give services such as kitchens, common rooms, and laundry facilities.

Price: Hostels can range in price from budget-friendly to luxury. Set a budget before you start your search so that you can find a hostel that fits your needs.

Here are a few tips for living in a hotel in France:

- **Book in advance:** Hostels can fill up quickly, especially during peak season. It is important to book your hotel in advance, especially if you are going during the summer months.
- **Be respectful of other guests:** Hostels are shared places, so it is important to be respectful of other guests. Keep noise to a minimum and clean up after yourself.
- **Be aware of your surroundings:** Hostels can be a target for pickpockets, so it is important to be aware of your surroundings and keep your things close to you.

Camping and hosteling are two great ways to travel on a budget and explore new cultures. By following these tips, you can have a safe and fun time camping or hosteling in France.

5

Must-Visit Destinations

Paris

Paris, the city of France, is one of the most famous vacation locations in the world. With its famous sites, gorgeous architecture, and lively culture, Paris has something to offer everyone.

Here are just a few of the things that make Paris so special:

Eiffel Tower:

The Eiffel Tower is one of the most famous sites in the world. It is a must-see for any guest to Paris.

Louvre Museum:

The Louvre Museum is one of the biggest and most famous museums in the world. It holds a huge collection of art, including the Mona Lisa.

Notre Dame church:

Notre Dame Cathedral is a beautiful Gothic church that is one of the most popular tourist attractions in Paris.

Arc de Triomphe:

The Arc de Triomphe is a magnificent arch that honors the wins of the French army. It is one of the most recognized buildings in Paris.

Sacré-Coeur church:

Sacré-Coeur Basilica is a white-domed church that offers amazing views of Paris.

Latin Quarter:

The Latin Quarter is a famous area in Paris that is known for its small streets, bars, and bookstores.

Montmartre:

Montmartre is a hilly neighborhood in Paris that is known for its artists, bars, and Sacré-Coeur Basilica.

Jardin du Luxembourg:

The Jardin du Luxembourg is a beautiful public park in Paris that is great for a relaxing walk.

Champs-Élysées:

The Champs-Élysées is a famous street in Paris that is known for its expensive shops and restaurants.

Paris is a city that has something to offer everyone. Whether you are interested in art, history, food, or simply want to experience the city's vibrant atmosphere, Paris has something for you.

Here are a few tips for planning your trip to Paris:

- Book your flights and accommodation in advance, especially if you are traveling during peak season.
- Purchase a Paris Pass to save money on admission to popular attractions.
- Learn a few basic French phrases.
- Be aware of your surroundings and keep your belongings close to you.
- Take your time and enjoy the city's many sights and attractions.

Paris is a magical city that is sure to leave a lasting impression on you. With its rich history, culture, and beauty, Paris is a must-visit destination for any traveler.

Île-de-France

Île-de-France is a region in north-central France. It is the most populous region in France, and it is home to the country's capital, Paris.

Île-de-France is a land of contrasts. It is home to both urban and rural areas, and it has a rich history that dates back centuries.

The region is known for its many historical landmarks, including the Palace of Versailles, the Château de Fontainebleau, and the Abbey of Saint-Denis. Île-de-France is also home to some of France's most famous museums, such as the Louvre Museum and the Musée d'Orsay.

In addition to its historical attractions, Île-de-France is also a popular destination for its natural beauty. The region is home to several forests, including the Forest of Fontainebleau and the Forest of Rambouillet. Île-de-France is also home to several rivers, including the Seine River and the Marne River.

Here are a few of the most popular tourist destinations in Île-de-France:

- **Paris:**

Paris is the capital of France and one of the most popular tourist destinations in the world. Paris is home to many iconic landmarks, such as the Eiffel Tower, the Louvre Museum, and the Notre Dame Cathedral.

- **Versailles:**

Versailles is a former royal residence located just outside of Paris. Versailles is known for its lavish gardens and its opulent palace.

- **Fontainebleau:**

Fontainebleau is another former royal residence located just outside of Paris. Fontainebleau is known for its Renaissance architecture and its beautiful gardens.

- **Château de Chantilly:**

The Château de Chantilly is a historic castle located in the Chantilly Forest.

The castle is known for its art collection and its gardens.

Château de Vincennes:

The Château de Vincennes is a medieval castle located in the eastern suburbs of Paris. The castle is known for its moat and its keep.

Île-de-France is a region with something to offer everyone. Whether you are interested in history, art, nature, or simply want to experience the vibrant atmosphere of Paris, Île-de-France has something for you.

Normandy

Normandy is a region in northwestern France. It is known for its beautiful coastline, its rolling countryside, and its rich history. Normandy was the site of the D-Day landings during World War II, and it is home to many historical landmarks related to the war.

Normandy is also a popular tourist destination for its natural beauty. The region is home to several beaches, cliffs, and forests. Normandy is also a popular destination for hikers, cyclists, and birdwatchers.

Here are a few of the most popular tourist destinations in Normandy:

Mont Saint-Michel:

Mont Saint-Michel is a tidal island located in the Bay of Saint-Michel. It is home to a Benedictine abbey, which is a UNESCO World Heritage Site.

D-Day beaches:

The D-Day beaches are a series of beaches located on the Normandy coast. These beaches were the site of the Allied landings on D-Day, June 6, 1944.

Bayeux Tapestry:

The Bayeux Tapestry is an embroidered cloth that tells the story of the Norman Conquest of England. It is one of the most famous tapestries in the world.

Honfleur:

Honfleur is a picturesque port town located on the Seine River. It is known for its narrow streets, its colorful houses, and its maritime atmosphere.

Etretat:

Étretat is a coastal town located in Normandy. It is known for its white cliffs, its chalk formations, and its beaches.

Normandy is a region with something to offer everyone. Whether you are interested in history, nature, or simply want to experience the charm of Normandy, you are sure to have a wonderful time.

Brittany

Brittany is a region in northwestern France. It is known for its rugged coastline, its picturesque villages, and its Celtic culture.

Brittany is a popular tourist destination for its natural beauty. The region is home to several beaches, cliffs, and forests. Brittany is also a popular destination for hikers, cyclists, and birdwatchers.

Here are a few of the most popular tourist destinations in Brittany:

Côte de Granit Rose:

The Côte de Granit Rose is a stretch of coastline located in northern Brittany. It is known for its pink granite cliffs and its turquoise waters.

Île de Sein:

Île de Sein is a small island located off the coast of Brittany. It is known for its picturesque harbor and its traditional way of life.

Fort La Latte:

Fort La Latte is a medieval castle located on a rocky outcrop on the coast of Brittany. It is a popular tourist destination for its stunning views and its historical significance.

Carnac:

Carnac is a town located in southern Brittany. It is known for its thousands of standing stones, which are thought to date back to the Neolithic period.

Quimper:

Quimper is a city located in southern Brittany. It is known for its pottery, its cathedral, and its historic center.

Brittany is also a region with a rich cultural heritage. The region is home to a number of Celtic festivals and traditions. Brittany is also known for its cuisine, which features seafood, cider, and crêpes.

Brittany is a region with something to offer everyone. Whether you are interested in history, nature, culture, or simply want to relax and enjoy the Breton way of life, you are sure to have a wonderful time in Brittany.

The Loire Valley

The Loire Valley is a region in central France that is known for its beautiful castles, its charming villages, and its rolling countryside. The region is also home to a number of vineyards, and it is a popular destination for wine tasting.

The Loire Valley was once the royal residence of France, and it is home to some of the most iconic castles in the country, including Château de Chambord, Château de Chenonceau, and Château d'Amboise. The castles are all open to the public, and they offer visitors a glimpse into the life of the French aristocracy.

In addition to its castles, the Loire Valley is also home to a number of charming villages. These villages are often overlooked by tourists, but they offer a glimpse into the traditional French way of life. Some of the most popular villages in the Loire Valley include Villandry, Amboise, and Chinon.

The Loire Valley is also home to a number of vineyards. The region is known for its production of red, white, and rosé wines. Visitors can enjoy wine tasting at many of the vineyards in the region.

The Loire Valley is a beautiful region with something to offer everyone. Whether you are interested in history, culture, wine, or simply want to relax and enjoy the French countryside, you are sure to have a wonderful time in the Loire Valley.

Here are a few more things to do in the Loire Valley:

- Visit the Château de Villandry, which is known for its beautiful gardens.
- Take a boat trip on the Loire River.
- Visit the town of Tours, which is the capital of the Loire Valley.
- Sample the local cuisine, which features fresh produce and regional specialties.
- Enjoy a picnic in one of the many parks or gardens in the Loire Valley.

The Loire Valley is a truly magical place, and it is a must-visit destination for anyone traveling to France.

Dordogne

The Dordogne is a region in southwestern France that is known for its beautiful countryside, its medieval villages, and its prehistoric cave paintings. The region is also home to a number of rivers and lakes, making it a popular destination for outdoor activities such as hiking, biking, and fishing.

The Dordogne is a region with a rich history. The region was once inhabited by prehistoric humans, and there are a number of cave paintings that have been discovered in the region. The region was also a major center of medieval culture, and there are a number of beautiful medieval villages that can be found in the Dordogne.

Some of the most popular tourist destinations in the Dordogne include:

Sarlat-la-Canéda:

Sarlat-la-Canéda is a medieval town that is known for its well-preserved historic center. The town is home to a number of shops, restaurants, and art galleries.

Les Eyzies-de-Tayac-Sireuil:

Les Eyzies-de-Tayac-Sireuil is a town that is known for its prehistoric cave paintings. The town is home to a number of museums and visitor centers that offer information on the cave paintings.

Pont du Gard:

Pont du Gard is an ancient Roman aqueduct that is located near the town of Vers-Pont-du-Gard. The aqueduct is one of the best-preserved Roman aqueducts in the world.

Lascaux Cave:

Lascaux Cave is a prehistoric cave that is known for its cave paintings. The cave is located near the town of Montignac.

Dordogne Valley:

The Dordogne Valley is a beautiful valley that is located in the heart of the Dordogne region. The valley is home to a number of villages, castles, and churches.

The Dordogne is a region with something to offer everyone. Whether you are interested in history, culture, nature, or simply want to relax and enjoy the French countryside, you are sure to have a wonderful time in the Dordogne.

Provence

Provence is a region in southeastern France that is known for its beautiful lavender fields, its picturesque villages, and its delicious cuisine. The region is also home to a number of historical sites, including the Roman ruins of Arles and the hilltop villages of Gordes and Roussillon.

Provence is a popular tourist destination, and it is easy to see why. The region has something to offer everyone, from history and culture lovers to nature enthusiasts and foodies.

Here are a few of the most popular tourist destinations in Provence:

- **Aix-en-Provence:**

Aix-en-Provence is a charming city that is known for its lively atmosphere, its beautiful architecture, and its many cafes and restaurants.

- **Cassis**:

Cassis is a picturesque fishing village that is located on the Mediterranean coast. The village is known for its beautiful harbor, its white-washed houses, and its delicious seafood.

- **Gordes:**

Gordes is a hilltop village that is known for its stunning views of the surrounding countryside. The village is also home to a number of art galleries and boutiques.

Roussillon:

Roussillon is a hilltop village that is known for its red and ochre cliffs. The village is also home to a number of salt pans, which are used to produce salt.

Les Baux-de-Provence:

Les Baux-de-Provence is a medieval village that is perched on a rocky outcrop. The village is known for its ruined castle, its narrow streets, and its stunning views of the surrounding countryside.

In addition to its beautiful scenery and charming villages, Provence is also known for its delicious cuisine. The region is known for its use of fresh, local ingredients, and its dishes are often influenced by Mediterranean cuisine. Some of the most popular dishes in Provence include ratatouille, bouillabaisse, and tapenade.

Provence is a region with something to offer everyone. Whether you are looking for a relaxing vacation, a cultural getaway, or a foodie paradise, Provence is the perfect destination for you.

French Riviera

The French Riviera, also known as the Côte d'Azur, is a region in southeastern France that is known for its beautiful coastline, its glamorous resorts, and its luxurious lifestyle. The region is also home to a number of historical sites, including the walled city of Nice and the medieval village of Eze.

The French Riviera is a popular tourist destination, and it is easy to see why. The region has something to offer everyone, from history and culture lovers to beach bums and fashionistas.

Here are a few of the most popular tourist destinations on the French Riviera:

Nice:

Nice is a charming city that is known for its beautiful beaches, its Old Town, and its lively atmosphere.

Monaco:

Monaco is a tiny principality that is known for its casinos, its luxury yachts, and its Formula One Grand Prix.

Saint-Tropez:

Saint-Tropez is a glamorous resort town that is known for its beautiful beaches, its celebrity sightings, and its chic boutiques.

Cannes:

Cannes is a cosmopolitan city that is known for its annual film festival, its beautiful beaches, and its luxury hotels.

Antibes:

Antibes is a charming town that is known for its beautiful harbor, its Picasso Museum, and its proximity to the Îles de Lérins, a group of two islands that are located just off the coast.

In addition to its beautiful beaches and glamorous resorts, the French Riviera is also home to a number of historical sites. Here are a few of the most popular historical sites on the French Riviera:

Walled City of Nice:

The Walled City of Nice is a medieval city that is located in the heart of Nice. The city is home to a number of narrow streets, old churches, and museums.

Medieval Village of Eze:

The Medieval Village of Eze is a hilltop village that is located overlooking the Mediterranean Sea. The village is home to a number of narrow streets, old buildings, and a botanical garden.

Chateau d'If:

Chateau d'If is a former prison that is located on an island just off the coast of Marseille. The castle is known for its role in Alexandre Dumas' novel "The Count of Monte Cristo."

The French Riviera is a region with something to offer everyone. Whether you are looking for a glamorous vacation, a historical getaway, or simply a chance to relax on the beach, the French Riviera is the perfect destination for you.

The French Alps

The French Alps are a mountain range that straddles the border between France and Italy. The range is home to some of the highest peaks in Europe, including Mont Blanc, the highest mountain in the Alps and the Western Hemisphere.

The French Alps are a popular tourist destination, and for good reason. The region offers something for everyone, from stunning scenery and outdoor activities to charming villages and delicious cuisine.

Here are a few of the most popular tourist destinations in the French Alps:

Chamonix:

Chamonix is a town that is located at the foot of Mont Blanc. The town is a popular base for mountaineering, skiing, and other outdoor activities.

Megève:

Megève is a luxury ski resort that is located in the Haute-Savoie department of France. The resort is known for its world-class skiing, its charming villages, and its Michelin-starred restaurants.

Annecy:

Annecy is a town that is located on the shores of Lake Annecy. The town is known for its beautiful canals, its picturesque old town, and its proximity to the Alps.

Grindelwald:

Grindelwald is a village that is located in the Bernese Oberland region of Switzerland. The village is a popular base for hiking, mountaineering, and skiing.

Zermatt:

Zermatt is a car-free village that is located in the Swiss Alps. The village is known for its stunning views of the Matterhorn and its world-class skiing.

In addition to its stunning scenery and outdoor activities, the French Alps are also home to a number of charming villages. Here are a few of the most popular villages in the French Alps:

Eze:

Eze is a hilltop village that is located overlooking the Mediterranean Sea. The village is known for its narrow streets, its colorful houses, and its botanical gardens.

Sainte-Agnès:

Sainte-Agnès is a medieval village that is located on a rocky outcrop in the Alpes-Maritimes department of France. The village is known for its stunning views of the surrounding countryside and its delicious food.

Gorges du Verdon:

The Gorges du Verdon is a canyon that is located in the Alpes-de-Haute-Provence department of France. The canyon is known for its turquoise waters and its dramatic cliffs.

Col du Galibier:

The Col du Galibier is a mountain pass that is located in the French Alps. The pass is known for its challenging climbs and its stunning views of the surrounding mountains.

The French Alps are a truly magical place. With their stunning scenery, outdoor activities, and charming villages, the French Alps have something to offer everyone.

6

Other Regions of France

Burgundy

Burgundy is an area in eastern France that is known for its beautiful scenery, its world-renowned wines, and its lovely towns. The area is also home to a number of important sites, including the Palace of the Dukes of Burgundy and the Collegiate Church of Notre-Dame.

Burgundy is a famous tourist location, and it is easy to see why. The area has something to offer everyone, from history and culture lovers to wine fans and eaters.

Here are a few of the most famous tourist spots in Burgundy:

Beaune:

Beaune is a charming town that is known for its wine production and its yearly wine auction.

Chablis:

Chablis is a town that is known for its white wines, which are made from the Chardonnay grape.

Meursault:

Meursault is a town that is known for its white wines, which are made from the Chardonnay grape.

Corton:

Corton is a town that is known for its red wines, which are made from the Pinot Noir grape.

Vosne-Romanée:

Vosne-Romanée is a village that is known for its red wines, which are made from the Pinot Noir grape.

In addition to its wine production, Burgundy is also known for its wonderful food. The area is known for its use of fresh, local products, and its recipes are often inspired by traditional French food. Some of the most famous meals in Burgundy include coq au vin, boeuf bourguignon, and escargots.

Burgundy is an area with something to offer everyone. Whether you are looking for a romance break, a food adventure, or a cultural experience, Burgundy is the right location for you.

Champagne

Champagne is an area in northeastern France that is known for its sparkling wine. The area is nestled in the foothills of the Ardennes Mountains and is home to over 15,000 acres of vines.

Champagne is a famous tourist location, and for good reason. The region offers something for everyone, from stunning scenery and outdoor activities to lovely towns and delicious food.

Here are a few of the most famous tourist spots in Champagne:

Reims:

Reims is a city that is known for its church, which is the site of many French coronations. The city is also home to a number of wine houses, including Moët & Chandon and Veuve Clicquot.

Épernay:

Épernay is a town that is known for its wine caves. The town is home to over 100 champagne houses, and tourists can take tours of the basements and learn about the champagne-making process.

Champagne-Ardenne Regional Natural Park:

The Champagne-Ardenne Regional Natural Park is a park that is found in the Champagne area. The park is home to rolling hills, woods, and wineries. Visitors can enjoy hikes, biking, and horseback rides in the park.

Aube:

The Aube department is located in the Champagne area. The department is home to a number of lovely towns, including Bar-sur-Aube and Chablis. Visitors can enjoy exploring the towns and tasting the local food.

Troyes:

Troyes is a city that is located in the Aube department. The city is known for its ancient buildings and its yearly Christmas market. Visitors can enjoy exploring the city's ancient center and shopping for Christmas gifts at the market.

In addition to its stunning scenery and outdoor activities, Champagne is also home to a number of lovely towns. Here are a few of the most famous towns in Champagne:

Châlons-en-Champagne:

Châlons-en-Champagne is a city that is known for its ancient center and its yearly Foire de Châlons, a trade fair that is held in September.

Mézières-sur-Seine:

Mézières-sur-Seine is a city that is known for its medieval castle and its yearly event d'Été, a summer event that features music, dance, and theater.

Bouzy:

Bouzy is a town that is known for its wine production. The village is home to a number of champagne houses, and tourists can take tours of the caves and learn about the champagne-making process.

Aÿ:

Aÿ is a town that is known for its wine production. The village is home to a number of champagne houses, and tourists can take tours of the caves and learn about the champagne-making process.

Hautvillers:

Hautvillers is a town that is known for its connection with Dom Pérignon, the monk who is credited with developing the champagne-making process. The village is home to a number of champagne houses, and tourists can take tours of the caves and learn about the champagne-making process.

Champagne is a truly beautiful place. With its stunning scenery, outdoor activities, lovely towns, and delicious food, Champagne has something to offer everyone.

Alsace

Alsace is an area in northeastern France that is known for its beautiful scenery, its delicious food, and its unique culture. The area is situated in the slopes of the Vosges Mountains and is home to a number of lovely towns, ancient castles, and world-renowned wineries.

Alsace is a famous vacation location, and for good reason. The region offers something for everyone, from stunning scenery and outdoor activities to lovely towns and delicious food.

Here are a few of the most famous vacation spots in Alsace:

Colmar:

Colmar is a charming town that is known for its canals, its half-timbered houses, and its Christmas markets.

Eguisheim:

Eguisheim is a town that is known for its beautiful streets, its wine cellars, and its yearly grape fair.

Ribeauvillé:

Ribeauvillé is a town that is known for its wine production, its medieval castle, and its annual wine fair.

Kaysersberg:

Kaysersberg is a town that is known for its small streets, its half-timbered houses, and its beautiful setting on the River Ill.

Strasbourg:

Strasbourg is a city that is known for its Gothic church, its European Parliament, and its Christmas market.

In addition to its stunning scenery and lovely towns, Alsace is also known for its wonderful food. The region is known for its use of fresh, local products, and its recipes are often inspired by German and Alsatian food. Some of the most famous meals in Alsace include **choucroute (sauerkraut), tarte flambée (Alsatian pizza), and baeckeoffe (a slow-cooked dish of meat and veggies).**

Alsace is also known for its world-renowned wines. The area provides a range of wines, including **riesling, gewurztraminer, and pinot noir**. Visitors to Alsace can enjoy wine tasting at a number of wineries in the area.

Alsace is a truly magical place. With its stunning scenery, lovely towns, delicious food, and world-renowned wines, Alsace has something to offer everyone.

Basque Country

The Basque Country is an area found in northern Spain and southwestern France. It is home to a unique society and language that is different from both Spanish and French. The Basque Country is also known for its beautiful scenery, its wonderful food, and its lively culture.

The Basque Country is a famous vacation location, and for good reason. The region offers something for everyone, from stunning scenery and outdoor activities to lovely towns and delicious food.

Here are a few of the most famous tourist spots in the Basque Country:

San Sebastián:

San Sebastián is a city that is known for its beautiful beaches, its Michelin-starred restaurants, and its yearly film festival.

Biarritz:

Biarritz is a vacation town that is known for its beautiful beaches, its gambling, and its surfing.

Guernica:

Guernica is a town that is known for its sad past and its beautiful church.

Oñati:

Oñati is a town that is known for its university, its ancient building, and its yearly jazz festival.

Hondarribia:

Hondarribia is a town that is known for its beautiful bay, its protected walls, and its delicious fish.

In addition to its stunning scenery and lovely towns, the Basque Country is also known for its wonderful food. The region is known for its use of fresh, local products, and its recipes are often inspired by traditional Basque food. Some of the most famous meals in the Basque Country include **pintxos (small tapas), txuleta (Basque steak), and marmitako (a fish stew).**

The Basque Country is also known for its lively culture. The area is home to a number of festivals and events throughout the year, including the San Sebastián Film Festival, the Azkena Rock Festival, and the Tamborrada Festival in San Sebastián.

The Basque Country is a truly beautiful place. With its stunning scenery, lovely towns, wonderful food, and lively culture, the Basque Country has something to offer everyone.

Corsica

Corsica is an island in the Mediterranean Sea that is located south of mainland France. It is known for its beautiful beauty, its rocky shoreline, and its unique culture.

Corsica is a famous vacation location, and for good reason. The island offers something for everyone, from stunning scenery and outdoor activities to lovely towns and delicious food.

Here are a few of the most famous vacation spots in Corsica:

Ajaccio:

Ajaccio is the capital of Corsica and is known for its beautiful beaches, its ancient center, and its connection with Napoleon Bonaparte.

Calvi:

Calvi is a town that is known for its beautiful harbor, its ancient castle, and its sandy beaches.

Porto-Vecchio:

Porto-Vecchio is a town that is known for its beautiful beaches, its busy nightlife, and its sailing.

L'Île Rousse:

L'Île Rousse is a town that is known for its white-sand beaches, its beautiful harbor, and its Corsican food.

Gorges de Spelunca:

The Gorges de Spelunca are a group of tunnels that are found in the northeast of Corsica. The gorges are known for their stunning scenery and their hiking trails.

In addition to its stunning scenery and charming villages, Corsica is also known for its delicious food. The island is known for its use of fresh, local ingredients, and its dishes are often influenced by traditional Corsican cuisine. Some of the most popular dishes in Corsica include **figatellu (Corsican sausage), brocciu (a type of Corsican cheese), and aziminu (a Corsican stew).**

Corsica is also known for its unique culture. The island has its own language, music, and dance. Visitors to Corsica can experience the island's unique culture by visiting its villages, festivals, and markets.

Corsica is a truly magical place. With its stunning scenery, charming villages, delicious food, and unique culture, Corsica has something to offer everyone.

7

Exploring French Cuisine

French Culinary Traditions

French cooking customs are some of the most recognized and loved in the world. French food is known for its luxury, its use of fresh, seasonal products, and its focus on taste and balance.

Here are some of the key traits of French cooking traditions:

Use of fresh, seasonal ingredients: French food is based on the use of fresh, seasonal products. This means that meals are made to highlight the natural tastes of the products. For example, a French cook might use fresh summer tomatoes to make a gazpacho soup, or fresh winter truffles to make a steak tartare.

Focus on taste and balance: French food is known for its focus on taste and balance. French cooks carefully consider the tastes of each item when making a dish. They also try to make meals that are both delicious and balanced. For example, a French cook might pair a sweet sauce with a salty meal to create a difference of tastes.

Emphasis on presentation: French food is also known for its focus on appearance. French cooks take great care to show their meals in a visually appealing way. This might involve using colored decorations, plating the food in a creative way, or even using special serving dishes.

Some of the most iconic French dishes include:

Coq au vin:

Coq au vin is a classic French dish of chicken braised in red wine. The dish is typically flavored with herbs and spices, such as thyme, rosemary, and bay leaves.

Boeuf bourguignon:

Boeuf bourguignon is another classic French dish of beef braised in red wine. The dish is typically flavored with herbs and spices, such as onions, carrots, and mushrooms.

Escargots:

Escargots are snails that are cooked in garlic butter and parsley. They are typically served as an appetizer.

Ratatouille:

Ratatouille is a vegetable stew that is made with eggplant, zucchini, tomatoes, onions, and garlic. It is typically served as a side dish.

Soupe à l'oignon:

Soupe à l'oignon is a French onion soup that is made with caramelized onions, beef broth, and topped with croutons and Gruyère cheese.

French culinary traditions are also known for their regional specialties. For example, the region of Brittany is known for its crêpes and galettes, while the region of Provence is known for its ratatouille and bouillabaisse.

French cuisine has had a major influence on cuisines around the world. Today, French culinary traditions are enjoyed by people from all walks of life, and French restaurants can be found in major cities all over the globe.

Here are some additional insights into French culinary traditions:

- **French cuisine is a social experience:** Meals in France are typically enjoyed with friends and family. French people take their time to eat and savor their food.
- **French cuisine is a celebration of local produce:** French chefs take pride in using the best local ingredients available. They support local farmers and suppliers, and they work to create dishes that showcase the unique flavors of their region.
- **French cuisine is a living tradition:** French culinary traditions are constantly evolving. French chefs are always experimenting with new ingredients and techniques. However, they always remain rooted in the traditional values of French cuisine, such as using fresh, seasonal ingredients and focusing on flavor and balance.

French culinary traditions are a rich and complex part of French culture. They are based on a deep appreciation for food and a commitment to quality. French cuisine is something to be savored and enjoyed.

Iconic French Dishes

French cuisine is renowned for its sophistication, elegance, and diversity. From classic dishes like coq au vin and ratatouille to more modern creations, French chefs have a knack for creating dishes that are both delicious and visually appealing. Here is a list of some of the most iconic French dishes:

- **Coq au vin**

Coq au vin is a classic French dish of chicken braised in red wine. The dish is typically flavored with herbs and spices, such as thyme, rosemary, and bay leaves. Coq au vin is often served with mashed potatoes or noodles.

- **Boeuf bourguignon**

Boeuf bourguignon is another classic French dish of beef braised in red wine. The dish is typically flavored with herbs and spices, such as onions, carrots, and mushrooms. Boeuf bourguignon is often served with mashed potatoes or noodles.

- **Escargots**

Escargots are snails that are cooked in garlic butter and parsley. They are typically served as an appetizer. Escargots are a popular dish in France and other parts of Europe.

- **Ratatouille**

Ratatouille is a vegetable stew that is made with eggplant, zucchini, tomatoes, onions, and garlic. It is typically served as a side dish. Ratatouille is a popular dish in France and other parts of the Mediterranean region.

Soupe à l'oignon

Soupe à l'oignon is a French onion soup that is made with caramelized onions, beef broth, and topped with croutons and Gruyère cheese. Soupe à l'oignon is a popular dish in France and other parts of Europe.

Steak tartare

Steak tartare is a dish of finely chopped raw beef that is typically served with a variety of condiments, such as capers, onions, and egg yolks. Steak tartare is a popular dish in France and other parts of Europe.

Crêpes

Crêpes are thin pancakes that can be served with either sweet or savory fillings. Sweet crêpes are often served with Nutella, fruit, or whipped cream. Savory crêpes are often filled with ham, cheese, or vegetables. Crêpes are a popular dish in France and other parts of Europe.

Bouillabaisse

Bouillabaisse is a seafood stew that is made with a variety of fish, shellfish, and vegetables. It is typically served with rouille, a garlicky mayonnaise. Bouillabaisse is a popular dish in the Provence region of France.

Macarons

Macarons are small, round cookies that are made with almond flour, egg whites, and sugar. They are typically filled with a ganache, buttercream, or jam. Macarons are a popular dessert in France and other parts of the world.

Crème brûlée

Crème brûlée is a custard dessert that is topped with a layer of caramelized sugar. It is typically served in a ramekin. Crème brûlée is a popular dessert in France and other parts of the world.

These are just a few of the many iconic French dishes. With its rich culinary history and diverse culinary traditions, France has something to offer everyone.

Dining Etiquette

Dining etiquette in France is important to the French people and is a reflection of their culture and values. While there are many different regional variations, there are some general rules that apply to dining in France.

Before the meal

- Arrive on time: Punctuality is important in France, and arriving late is considered rude.
- Greet your host and other guests with a handshake or kiss on the cheek.
- If you are bringing a gift, such as flowers or wine, present it to your host as soon as you arrive.
- Wait to be seated by your host.
- Sit up straight and keep your hands on the table.
- Do not unfold your napkin until you are seated.
- Place your napkin on your lap once you are seated.

During the meal

- Use the correct utensils: French meals typically consist of multiple courses, each of which has its own designated utensils. Be sure to use the correct utensils for each course.
- Eat with your knife and fork in your right and left hands, respectively.
- Do not cut your food into small pieces all at once. Instead, cut off one bite at a time.
- Do not talk with your mouth full.
- Take small bites and chew thoroughly.
- Do not slurp your soup.
- Do not rest your elbows on the table.
- Do not play with your food or utensils.
- Do not eat your bread until the main course arrives.
- Wait until everyone at the table has finished eating before leaving.

After the meal

- Thank your host for the meal.
- Place your napkin on the table to the right of your plate.
- If you are drinking coffee, place your spoon in the saucer to the right of the cup.
- If you are drinking tea, place your spoon in the saucer to the right of the cup.
- If you are staying with your host overnight, offer to help with the dishes.

Here are some additional tips for dining etiquette in France:

- It is polite to try everything that is served to you.
- If you have any dietary restrictions, be sure to let your host know in advance.
- If you are unsure of how to eat a particular dish, ask your host for assistance.
- Do not be afraid to ask questions about the food: The French people are proud of their cuisine and are happy to talk about it.
- Relax and enjoy the meal! Dining in France should be a pleasant and enjoyable experience.

By following these general rules of dining etiquette, you will show your respect for French culture and tradition.

Food and Wine Regions

France is a country with a rich and diverse culinary history. Each region of France has its own unique cuisine, which is influenced by the region's climate, geography, and culture. Here is a guide to some of the most famous food and wine regions in France:

Alsace

Alsace is a region in northeastern France that is known for its beautiful villages, its medieval castles, and its world-renowned wines. Alsace is also known for its delicious food, which is influenced by both French and German cuisine. Some of the most popular dishes in Alsace include **choucroute (sauerkraut), tarte flambée (Alsatian pizza), and baeckeoffe (a slow-cooked dish of meat and vegetables)**. Alsace is also known for its white wines, such as riesling and gewurztraminer.

Bordeaux

Bordeaux is a region in southwestern France that is known for its world-renowned wines. Bordeaux is also home to a number of charming villages, medieval castles, and Michelin-starred restaurants. Some of the most popular dishes in Bordeaux include **canelé (a small custard cake), magret de canard (duck breast), and entrecôte (rib steak)**. Bordeaux is also known for its red wines, such as cabernet sauvignon and merlot.

Burgundy

Burgundy is a region in eastern France that is known for its beautiful countryside, its world-renowned wines, and its charming villages. Burgundy is also home to a number of historical sites, such as the Palace of the Dukes of Burgundy and the Collegiate Church of Notre-Dame. Some of the most popular dishes in Burgundy include **coq au vin, boeuf bourguignon, and escargots**. Burgundy is also known for its red wines, such as pinot noir and gamay.

Champagne

Champagne is a region in northeastern France that is known for its sparkling wine. Champagne is also home to a number of charming villages, medieval castles, and Michelin-starred restaurants. Some of the most popular dishes in Champagne include **jambon de Reims (Reims ham), andouillette (a type of sausage), and boudin blanc (white sausage)**. Champagne is also known for its sparkling wine, which is made from chardonnay, pinot noir, and meunier grapes.

Loire Valley

The Loire Valley is a region in central France that is known for its beautiful scenery, its medieval castles, and its world-renowned wines. The Loire Valley is also home to a number of charming villages, historical sites, and Michelin-starred restaurants. Some of the most popular dishes in the Loire Valley include **rillettes de Tours (pork rillettes), crottin de Chavignol (goat cheese), and tarte Tatin (apple tart).** The Loire Valley is also known for its white wines, such as sauvignon blanc and chenin blanc.

Provence

Provence is a region in southeastern France that is known for its beautiful coastline, its charming villages, and its delicious food. Provence is also known for its rosé wines, which are made from grenache, cinsault, and syrah grapes. Some of the most popular dishes in Provence include **ratatouille, bouillabaisse, and soupe au pistou (pistou soup).** Provence is also known for its olive oil and its lavender.

Rhône Valley

The Rhône Valley is a region in southeastern France that is known for its beautiful scenery, its world-renowned wines, and its charming villages. The Rhône Valley is also home to a number of historical sites and Michelin-starred restaurants. Some of the most popular dishes in the Rhône Valley include **tapenade (olive tapenade), daube de boeuf (beef stew), and quenelles de brochet (pike quenelles).** The Rhône Valley is also known for its red wines, such as syrah and grenache, and its white wines, such as viognier and marsanne.

These are just a few of the many food and wine regions in France. With its rich culinary history and diverse culinary traditions, France has something to offer everyone.

8

Cultural Experiences

Museums and Art Galleries

France is home to some of the world's most famous museums and art galleries. From the Louvre Museum to the Musée d'Orsay, tourists can experience a wide range of art, from old items to modern works.

Here is a list of some of the most famous museums and art spaces in France:

Louvre Museum:

The Louvre Museum is the world's biggest museum and is home to a huge collection of art and objects from around the world. Some of the most famous works of art in the Louvre include the Mona Lisa, Venus de Milo, and Winged Victory of Samothrace.

Musée d'Orsay:

The Musée d'Orsay is situated in a former train station and houses a collection of Impressionist and Post-Impressionist art. Some of the most famous artists featured in the Musée d'Orsay include Monet, Renoir, Van Gogh, and Cézanne.

Centre Pompidou:

The Centre Pompidou is a modern and contemporary art museum that houses a collection of over 100,000 works of art. Some of the most famous artists featured in the Centre Pompidou include Picasso, Matisse, and Warhol.

Musée Rodin:

The Musée Rodin is a museum dedicated to the work of Auguste Rodin, one of the most famous artists of all time. The museum features a collection of over 6,000 works of art, including The Thinker and The Kiss.

Musée Picasso:

The Musée Picasso is a museum dedicated to the work of Pablo Picasso, one of the most important artists of the 20th century. The museum houses a collection of over 5,000 works of art, including paintings, sculptures, and drawings.

Musée de l'Orangerie:

The Musée de l'Orangerie is a museum that houses a collection of Impressionist and Post-Impressionist art. The museum is best known for its collection of eight Water Lilies paintings by Monet.

Musée Marmottan Monet:

The Musée Marmottan Monet is a museum that houses a collection of works by Claude Monet. The museum is also home to a collection of Impressionist and Post-Impressionist art by other artists, such as Renoir, Degas, and Sisley.

Palace of Versailles:

The Palace of Versailles is a former royal home that is now a museum. The castle is home to a collection of art and items from the French royalty.

Musée des Beaux-Arts de Lyon:

The Musée des Beaux-Arts de Lyon is a museum that houses a collection of art from the Middle Ages to the present day. The museum is home to works of art by artists such as Rubens, Rembrandt, and Van Gogh.

Musée des Confluences:

The Musée des Confluences is a science and culture museum that houses a collection of items from around the world. The museum is known for its unique design and its engaging displays.

Musée Matisse:

The Musée Matisse is a museum dedicated to the work of Henri Matisse, one of the most important artists of the 20th century. The museum houses a collection of over 1,000 works of art, including paintings, sculptures, and drawings.

Musée Marc Chagall:

The Musée Marc Chagall is a museum dedicated to the work of Marc Chagall, one of the most important artists of the 20th century. The museum houses a collection of over 800 works of art, including paintings, statues, and stained glass.

These are just a few of the many museums and art spaces in France. With its rich cultural history, France has something to give everyone who is interested in art.

Theaters and Performances

France has a long and rich background of theater and performance. From the opulent halls of Paris to the private stages of the provinces, there is something for everyone to enjoy.

Here is a list of some of the most popular shows and events in France:

Opera

Palais Garnier: The Palais Garnier is the home of the Paris Opera and is one of the most famous opera houses in the world. The Palais Garnier is known for its beautiful design and its world-class opera shows.

Opéra Bastille: The Opéra Bastille is another major opera house in Paris. The Opéra Bastille is known for its modern design and its wide program of opera concerts.

Opéra National de Bordeaux: The Opéra National de Bordeaux is the largest opera house in Bordeaux. The Opéra National de Bordeaux is known for its beautiful building and its high-quality opera shows.

Opéra de Lyon: The Opéra de Lyon is the largest opera house in Lyon. The Opéra de Lyon is known for its varied schedule of opera shows and its commitment to modern opera.

Theater

Comédie-Française: The Comédie-Française is the official theater of France. The Comédie-Française is known for its readings of famous French plays.

Théâtre de l'Odéon: The Théâtre de l'Odéon is another major theater in Paris. The Théâtre de l'Odéon is known for its wide schedule of plays and its commitment to modern theater.

Théâtre du Châtelet: The Théâtre du Châtelet is a big theater in Paris that is known for its plays and variety shows.

Théâtre des Bouffes Parisiens: The Théâtre des Bouffes Parisiens is a theater in Paris that is known for its shows and plays.

Théâtre de la Gaîté Montparnasse: The Théâtre de la Gaîté Montparnasse is a theater in Paris that is known for its modern theater and dance shows.

Other Performances

Moulin Rouge: The Moulin Rouge is a nightclub show in Paris that is known for its cancan dancers and its lively atmosphere.

Crazy Horse: The Crazy Horse is another cabaret show in Paris that is known for its beautiful dancers and its elaborate outfits.

Lido de Paris: The Lido de Paris is a nightclub show in Paris that is known for its large-scale production pieces and its special effects.

Cirque du Soleil: The Cirque du Soleil is a Canadian circus group that acts in different places around the world, including France. The Cirque du Soleil is known for its gymnastic shows and its amazing images.

Théâtre de l'Athénée-Louis-Jouvet: The Théâtre de l'Athénée-Louis-Jouvet is a theater in Paris that is known for its performances of modern plays and musicals. The theater is also home to the Théâtre des Variétés, which is a smaller theater that is known for its plays and revues.

These are just a few of the many shows and events in France. With its rich cultural history, France has something to offer everyone who is interested in the performing arts.

Festivals and Events

France is a country with a rich cultural history, and this is represented in the many holidays and events that take place throughout the year. From traditional folk fairs to world-renowned film events, there is something for everyone to enjoy.

Here is a list of some of the most famous parties and events in France:

Event d'Avignon:

The Festival d'Avignon is a theater event that takes place every year in the city of Avignon. The event is known for its world-class theater acts and its lively environment.

Cannes Film Festival:

The Cannes Film Festival is one of the most famous film events in the world. The festival takes place every year in the city of Cannes and is known for its red carpet glamour and its exclusive showing of new films.

Bastille Day:

Bastille Day is the French national holiday and is marked on July 14th every year. The day celebrates the breaking of the Bastille jail in 1789, which was a turning point in the French Revolution. Bastille Day is marked with parades, fireworks, and other events throughout France.

Fête de la Musique:

The Fête de la Musique is a music event that takes place every year on June 21st. The festival is marked with free music and acts in public places throughout France.

Tour de France:

The Tour de France is a bicycle race that takes place every year in July. The race is one of the most famous sports events in the world and covers a journey of over 2,000 miles. The Tour de France is known for its difficult terrain and its passionate fans.

Nice fair:

The Nice Carnival is a fair that takes place every year in the city of Nice. The fair is known for its bright floats, its elaborate outfits, and its lively atmosphere.

Menton Lemon event:

The Menton Lemon Festival is an event that takes place every year in the city of Menton. The fair celebrates the lemon harvest and includes statues, parades, and other events made from lemons.

Festival of Lights:

The event of Lights is an event that takes place every year in the city of Lyon. The festival marks the Feast of the Immaculate Conception and features light shows, music, and other events throughout the city.

Alsace Christmas Markets:

The Alsace Christmas Markets are a series of Christmas markets that take place in different towns and villages in the Alsace area of France. The markets are known for their lively mood, their wonderful food, and their beautiful Christmas displays.

Bordeaux Wine Festival:

The Bordeaux Wine event is an event that takes place every year in the city of Bordeaux. The festival celebrates the Bordeaux wine area and features wine tastes, wine parties, and other events.

Marseille International Film Festival:

The Marseille International Film event is a film event that takes place every year in the city of Marseille. The festival is known for its attention on independent pictures and its foreign selection of films.

These are just a few of the many fairs and events that take place in France throughout the year. With its rich cultural history, France has something to offer everyone who is looking for a unique and amazing experience.

Historical Sites

France is a country with a rich and varied past, and this is mirrored in the many historical places that are found throughout the country. From old Roman ruins to medieval castles to World War II sites, there is something for everyone to explore.

Here is a list of some of the most famous historical places in France:

- **Eiffel Tower:**

The Eiffel Tower is a wrought-iron lattice tower on the Champ de Mars in Paris, France. It is one of the most familiar buildings in the world and is one of the most famous tourist sites in France.

- **Palace of Versailles:**

The Palace of Versailles was the main royal home of France from 1682 to 1789. It is situated in the town of Versailles, just west of Paris. The castle is known for its lavish design and its beautiful grounds.

- **Mont Saint-Michel:**

Mont Saint-Michel is a tidal island and town in Normandy, northwestern France. It is situated about 1 kilometer (0.62 mi) off the coast, about 10 kilometers (6.2 mi) west of mainland France. The island is home to a Benedictine abbey, which is one of the most famous tourist sites in France.

- **Notre Dame Cathedral:**

Notre Dame church is an ancient Catholic church on the Île de la Cité in the fourth district of Paris, France. The church is generally thought to be one of the best examples of French Gothic design.

Arc de Triomphe:

The Arc de Triomphe is a grandiose arch in the 8th arrondissement of Paris, France. It is situated at the western end of the Champs-Élysées, which crosses the Place Charles de Gaulle, formerly the Place de l'Étoile. The arch honors the successes of the French army under Napoleon I.

Pont du Gard:

The Pont du Gard is an old Roman bridge that is located in the town of Vers-Pont-du-Gard in the Gard department of southern France. The aqueduct was built in the 1st century AD and is one of the best-preserved Roman aqueducts in the world.

D-Day Beaches:

The D-Day Beaches are the beaches in Normandy where Allied forces landed on June 6, 1944, during World War II. The beaches are now popular tourist sites and are home to a number of museums and shrines.

Carcassonne:

Carcassonne is a walled city in the Aude department of southern France. The city is known for its ancient defenses and its beautiful building.

Les Invalides:

Les Invalides is a collection of buildings in the 7th arrondissement of Paris, France. The building includes a hospital, a museum, and a church. The church is the resting place of Napoleon Bonaparte.

Sainte-Chapelle:

Sainte-Chapelle is a royal church in the Gothic style found on the Île de la Cité in the center of Paris. It was built by King Louis IX of France to house his collection of relics, including a piece of the Crown of Thorns.

Panthéon:

The Panthéon is a building in the Latin Quarter of Paris, France. It was originally built as a church, but it is now a tomb for famous French people. The Panthéon is the burial place of many important French people, including Voltaire, Victor Hugo, and Marie Curie.

These are just a few of the many ancient places that are found in France. With its rich and diverse history, France has something to offer everyone who is interested in learning more about the past.

9

Outdoor Adventures

Hiking and Trekking

France is a hiker's dream, with a wide range of tracks to suit all skills and hobbies. From the rocky peaks of the Alps to the rolling hills of Provence, there is something for everyone to enjoy.

Here are a few of the most famous hiking and walking locations in France:

The Alps:

The Alps are home to some of the most famous hiking trails in the world, including the Tour du Mont Blanc, a 104-mile trail that circumnavigates Mont Blanc, the highest peak in the Alps. Other popular hiking trails in the Alps include the Chamonix Valley, the Ecrins National Park, and the Vanoise National Park.

The Pyrenees:

The Pyrenees Mountains form a natural border between France and Spain.

The mountains are home to a variety of hiking trails, ranging from easy day hikes to difficult multi-day treks. Some of the most famous hiking trails in the Pyrenees include the Cirque de Gavarnie, the Pic du Midi d'Ossau, and the Carros de Foc.

Corsica:

The island of Corsica is situated in the Mediterranean Sea, just off the coast of France. Corsica is known for its stunning scenery, including rocky mountains, crystal-clear seas, and charming towns. Some of the most famous hiking trails in Corsica include the GR20, a difficult 112-mile trail that spans the length of the island, and the Mare a Mare Centre, a 107-mile trail that circles the center area of Corsica.

Provence:

Provence is an area in southeastern France known for its lavender fields, lovely towns, and Roman ruins. Provence is also a great place to go hiking. Some of the most famous hiking trails in Provence include the Calanques National Park, the Luberon Regional Nature Park, and the Alpilles Mountains.

No matter what your climbing skill or hobbies are, you are sure to find a trail in France that is great for you. Here are a few tips for planning your hike trip to France:

Choose the right time of year to go: The best time to go camping in France is during the spring (May-June) or fall (September-October), when the weather is warm.

Be prepared for all types of weather: The weather in France can be unexpected, so it is important to be prepared for all types of weather situations. Be sure to pack rain gear, sunscreen, and a hat.

Bring plenty of water and snacks: It is important to stay refreshed and fed while climbing, so be sure to bring plenty of water and food.

Tell someone where you are going: It is always a good idea to tell someone where you are going and when you expect to be back. This is especially important if you are going alone.

Respect the environment: Please be respectful of the environment and leave no sign.

With its beautiful scenery and wide range of tracks, France is a great place to go climbing and exploring. With a little planning, you can have an amazing hiking experience in France.

Skiing and Winter Sports

France is a world-renowned location for skiing and winter sports, with over 400 ski areas to choose from. From the famous peaks of the Alps to the lesser-known Pyrenees, there is something for everyone, from newcomers to pros.

Here are a few of the most famous skiing and winter sports locations in France:

The Alps:

The Alps are home to some of the most famous ski areas in the world, including Chamonix, Val d'Isère, and Courchevel. These areas offer a range of scenery, from easy hills for newbies to difficult runs for pros.

The Pyrenees:

The Pyrenees Mountains form a natural border between France and Spain. The mountains are home to a range of ski areas, including Grandvalira and

Baqueira Beret. These towns offer a more relaxed attitude than the Alps, and they are also more cheap.

Jura Mountains:

The Jura Mountains are found in eastern France. The mountains are home to a number of ski areas, including Les Rousses and Métabief. These resorts are smaller and less busy than the resorts in the Alps, but they offer a range of slopes for all types of skiers and riders.

Vosges Mountains:

The Vosges Mountains are found in northeastern France. The mountains are home to a number of ski areas, including La Bresse and Gérardmer. These locations are great for families and newbies, as they offer mostly easy hills.

In addition to skiing and snowboarding, there are a number of other winter sports that can be enjoyed in France, such as cross-country skiing, hiking, and ice skating. Many of the ski areas also offer a range of other sports, such as tubing, sliding, and dog running.

Here are a few tips for planning your skiing and winter sports trip to France:

Book your hotel and lift tickets in advance: This is especially important if you are going during peak season.

Be prepared for all types of weather: The weather in the mountains can be unexpected, so it is important to be prepared for all kinds of weather conditions. Be sure to pack warm clothes, sunscreen, and shades.

Rent your equipment: If you are not bringing your own equipment, you can rent it from most ski areas.

Take lessons: If you are a beginner, it is a good idea to take lessons from a skilled teacher.

Be aware of your surroundings: When skiing or snowboarding, it is important to be aware of your surroundings and to ski or snowboard within your limits.

With its beautiful scenery and wide range of ski areas, France is a great place to enjoy winter sports. With a little planning, you can have an amazing winter sports holiday in France.

Beaches and Water Sports

France is a country with a beautiful shore, and its beaches are some of the most popular in Europe. From the smooth beaches of the Riviera to the rocky coves of Brittany, there is something for everyone.

Here are a few of the most famous beaches in France:

> **Plage de Pampelonne, Ramatuelle:**

Plage de Pampelonne is a long stretch of sandy beach found on the French Riviera. The beach is known for its crystal-clear water and its beautiful setting.
   Plage de Palombaggia, Porto-Vecchio:
   Plage de Palombaggia is a beach found on the island of Corsica. The beach is known for its white sand and its blue waves.

> **Plage d'Étretat, Étretat:**

Plage d'Étretat is a pebble beach found in Normandy. The beach is known for its stunning rocks and its beautiful views.

Plage de la Grande Conche, Royan:

Plage de la Grande Conche is a sandy beach found on the Atlantic coast of France. The beach is known for its long stretch of sand and its lively atmosphere.

Plage de la Côte des Basques, Biarritz:

Plage de la Côte des Basques is a sandy beach found on the Basque coast of France. The beach is known for its big waves and its surfing culture.

France is also a great place to enjoy water sports. There are a number of companies that offer water sports activities, such as kayaking, swimming, sailing, and kitesurfing. Some of the most famous water sports locations in France include:

Calanques National Park:

The Calanques National Park is situated on the Mediterranean coast of France. The park is known for its beautiful scenery, which includes blue waves, limestone hills, and isolated coves. The park is a great place to enjoy sailing, swimming, and fishing.

Golfe du Morbihan:

The Golfe du Morbihan is a bay found on the Atlantic coast of France. The bay is known for its tide islands and its beautiful scenery. The Golfe du Morbihan is a great place to enjoy sailing, windsurfing, and kitesurfing.

Cannes:

Cannes is a city located on the French Riviera. Cannes is known for its yearly film festival and its beautiful beaches. Cannes is also a great place to enjoy water sports, such as jet skiing, paragliding, and scuba diving.

Biarritz:

Biarritz is a city located on the Basque coast of France. Biarritz is known for its big waves and its surfing culture. Biarritz is also a great place to enjoy other water sports, such as bodyboarding and stand-up paddleboarding.

No matter what your interests are, you are sure to find a beach or water sports spot in France that is great for you. With its beautiful shoreline and wide range of activities, France is a great place to enjoy a summer holiday.

Here are a few tips for planning your beach and water sports trip to France:

Choose the right time of year to go: The best time to visit the beaches in France is during the summer months (July-August), when the weather is warm and sunny.

Book your accommodation in advance: This is especially important if you are traveling during peak season.

Be prepared for crowds: The beaches in France can be very crowded during the summer months.

Pack sunscreen, sunglasses, and a hat: The sun can be very strong in France, so it is important to protect yourself from the sun's dangerous rays.

Be aware of the tides: The tides can be very strong in some places of France, so it is important to be aware of them before you go swimming.

With a little planning, you can have a wonderful beach and water sports holiday in France.

Cycling and Cycling Routes

France is a cyclist's dream, with a wide range of riding routes to choose from, ranging from easy rides along canals and rivers to difficult hills in the Alps and Pyrenees. Whether you are a casual rider or a serious road biker, you are sure to find a riding route in France that is great for you.

Here are a few of the most popular bike routes in France:

La Vélodyssée:

La Vélodyssée is a 1,250-kilometer bike route that runs along the Atlantic coast of France from Roscoff in Brittany to Hendaye in the Basque Country. The path is mostly flat and off-road, making it a great choice for riders of all types.

La Loire à Vélo:

La Loire à Vélo is an 800-kilometer bicycle route that follows the Loire River from Nevers to Saint-Brevin-les-Pins. The route is mostly flat and off-road, and it goes through some of the most beautiful scenery in France.

Canal du Midi:

The Canal du Midi is a 240-kilometer bicycle route that follows the Canal du Midi, a UNESCO World Heritage Site. The route is mostly flat and off-road, and it goes through some of the most beautiful towns in France.

ViaRhôna:

The ViaRhôna is an 815-kilometer bicycle route that follows the Rhône River from Lake Geneva to the Mediterranean Sea. The route is mostly flat and off-road, and it goes through some of the most famous wine areas in France.

EuroVelo 6:

EuroVelo 6 is a 3,653-kilometer bicycle route that runs from Saint-Nazaire in France to Constanța in Romania. The route goes through several countries in Western Europe, and it is a great choice for riders who want to experience different cultures.

In addition to these long-distance riding routes, there are also a number of shorter cycling routes in France that are great for day trips or weekend breaks. Here are a few examples:

The Seine Valley:

The Seine Valley is a beautiful area located just outside of Paris. There are a number of bicycle paths that wind through the valley, going through beautiful towns and farms.

The Loire Valley:

The Loire Valley is another beautiful area found in central France. There are a number of riding tracks that follow the Loire River and pass through some of the most famous castles in France, such as Chambord and Chenonceau.

The French Riviera:

The French Riviera is situated on the Mediterranean coast of France. There are a number of bicycle paths that hug the shoreline and pass through some of the most famous tourist locations in France, such as Nice, Cannes, and Saint-Tropez.

No matter what your fitness level or interests are, you are sure to find a bike route in France that is great for you. With its beautiful scenery and wide range of routes, France is a great place to enjoy a bicycle holiday.

Here are a few tips for planning your bike trip to France:

Choose the right time of year to go: The best time to bike in France is during the spring (May-June) or fall (September-October), when the weather is warm.

Book your hotel in advance: This is especially important if you are going during peak season.

Be prepared for all types of weather: The weather in France can be unexpected, so it is important to be prepared for all types of weather situations. Be sure to pack wet clothes, sunscreen, and a hat.

Bring plenty of water and food: It is important to stay refreshed and fed while riding, so be sure to bring plenty of water and snacks.

Tell someone where you are going: It is always a good idea to tell someone where you are going and when you expect to be back. This is especially important if you are riding alone.

Respect the environment: Please be respectful of the earth and leave no sign.

With a little planning, you can have an amazing cycling holiday in France.

10

Shopping in France

Souvenirs and Gifts

France is a country with a rich culture and past, and this is represented in the wide range of items and gifts that are available to buy. From traditional French food and drink to unique goods and artwork, there is something for everyone to find.

Here are a few of the most popular items and gifts from France:

Food and Drink:

France is known for its delicious food and drink, and there are many different things that you can buy to take home with you. Some common food gifts include cookies, candies, and cheese. You can also buy French drinks and spirits to enjoy at home.

Handicrafts:

France is home to a number of skilled artists who make unique products. Some famous arts include pots, glassware, and fabrics. You can also find a range of handmade jewelry and items.

Artwork:

France has a long and rich past of art, and there are many different shops and museums where you can buy artwork. Some famous French artists include Picasso, Monet, and Van Gogh. You can also buy copies and replicas of famous French art.

Other Souvenirs:

In addition to the things mentioned above, there are a number of other presents and gifts that you can buy in France. Some famous things include Eiffel Tower models, French flags, and letters. You can also find a variety of gifts with French words and sayings.

No matter what your income or interests are, you are sure to find a souvenir or gift from France that is great for you. With its rich culture and past, France has something to offer everyone.

Here are a few tips for shopping for presents and gifts in France:

Start your shopping early: The best items and gifts can sell out quickly, so it is important to start your shopping early.

Shop around: There are many different places to buy items and gifts in France, so it is important to shop around and compare prices.

Don't be afraid to bargain: Bargaining is popular in some places of France, so don't be afraid to try to get a good deal.

Be aware of the customs regulations: There are some limits on what you can bring back into your country from France, so be sure to check the customs rules before you journey.

With a little planning, you can have a wonderful time shopping for souvenirs and gifts in France.

Local Markets

France is a country with a rich cooking history, and its local markets are a great place to experience the freshest and best food that the country has to offer. From farmers markets to junk markets, there is something for everyone to enjoy.

Here are a few of the most popular neighborhood markets in France:

- **Marché d'Aligre, Paris:**

The Marché d'Aligre is a busy market located in the 12th arrondissement of Paris. The market is known for its wide range of fresh vegetables, meats, and cheeses. You can also find a range of cooked foods and snacks at the market.

- **Marché de Rungis, Rungis:**

The Marché de Rungis is the biggest trade market in the world. The market is located just outside of Paris, and it is open to the public on weekends. You can find a wide range of fresh vegetables, meats, and cheeses at the market.

- **Marché aux Puces de Saint-Ouen, Paris:**

The Marché aux Puces de Saint-Ouen is a flea market found in the northern suburbs of Paris. The market is known for its wide range of antiques, old clothes, and souvenirs.

Marché de la Croix-Rousse, Lyon:

The Marché de la Croix-Rousse is a market located in the Croix-Rousse area of Lyon. The market is known for its fresh vegetables, meats, and cheeses. You can also find a range of cooked foods and snacks at the market.

Marché du Cours Saleya, Nice:

The Marché du Cours Saleya is a flower and vegetable market found in the Old Town of Nice. The market is known for its bright flowers and its fresh food. You can also find a range of cooked foods and snacks at the market.

These are just a few of the many town markets in France. With its rich food history, France has something to offer everyone who is looking for a unique and memorable market experience.

Here are a few tips for visiting neighborhood markets in France:

Come early: The best veggies and meats sell out quickly, so it is important to come early.

Bring cash: Many sellers at area markets do not accept credit cards.

Be prepared to bargain: Bargaining is popular at local markets, so don't be afraid to try to get a good deal.

Be patient: Local markets can be busy and hectic, so it is important to be patient and understanding.

With a little planning, you can have a wonderful time visiting local markets in

France.

High-End Shopping

France is a mecca for high-end shopping, with a wide range of expensive shops and department stores spread throughout the country. From the famous Champs-Élysées in Paris to the glamorous Croisette in Cannes, there is something for everyone who is looking for a truly special shopping experience.

Here are a few of the most popular high-end shopping places in France:

Champs-Élysées, Paris:

The Champs-Élysées is one of the most famous streets in the world, and it is also home to a number of high-end luxury shops. Some of the most popular names on the Champs-Élysées include Chanel, Dior, Louis Vuitton, and Hermès.

Avenue Montaigne, Paris:

Avenue Montaigne is a chic street found in the 8th neighborhood of Paris. The street is known for its high-end clothes shops and its luxury hotels. Some of the most famous names on Avenue Montaigne include Valentino, Gucci, and Prada.

Place Vendôme, Paris:

Place Vendôme is a square found in the 1st district of Paris. The square is known for its high-end gold shops and its luxury hotels. Some of the most famous names on Place Vendôme include Cartier, Boucheron, and Van Cleef & Arpels.

Galeries Lafayette, Paris:

Galeries Lafayette is a department store located in the 9th district of Paris. The store is known for its wide range of high-end names and its beautiful design. Some of the most famous names at Galeries Lafayette include Chanel, Dior, and Louis Vuitton.

Printemps Haussmann, Paris:

Printemps Haussmann is a department store located in the 9th district of Paris. The store is known for its wide range of high-end names and its beautiful design. Some of the most famous names at Printemps Haussmann include Chanel, Dior, and Louis Vuitton.

La Croisette, Cannes:

La Croisette is a street located along the Mediterranean Sea in Cannes. The street is known for its high-end shops, its luxury hotels, and its yearly film festival. Some of the most famous names on La Croisette include Chanel, Dior, and Louis Vuitton.

In addition to the places mentioned above, there are a number of other high-end shopping destinations in France, such as **Saint-Tropez, Courchevel, and Megève**.

Here are a few tips for high-end shopping in France:

Do your research: Before you go shopping, it is important to do your research and find out which names are offered at which shops. You can also check the websites of the names you are interested in to see if they have any sales or special deals going on.

Be prepared to spend money: High-end shopping in France can be expensive, so be prepared to spend money. It is also important to keep in mind that some shops may require a minimum buy amount.

Dress appropriately: High-end shops in France tend to have a dress code, so it is important to dress properly. This means dressing in smart and well-fitting clothes.

Be nice and respectful: The staff at high-end stores in France are usually very knowledgeable and helpful. Be sure to be nice and respectful to them, and they will be happy to help you.

With a little planning, you can have a wonderful time high-end shopping in France.

Antique Hunting

France is a treasure trove for antique hunters, with a rich history and culture that goes back centuries. From street markets to unique shops, there is something for everyone to find.

Here are a few tips for treasure buying in France:

Do your research: Before you go, it is important to do your study and learn about the different types of antiques that are available in France. This will help you to cut down your search and make the most of your time.

Know where to look: There are many different places to find antiques in France, including street markets, specialty shops, and sale houses. Flea markets are a great place to find a wide variety of antiques at a variety of prices. Specialty shops are a good place to find high-quality antiques, but they can be more expensive. Auction houses are a good place to find rare and expensive antiques, but they can be very competitive.

Be prepared to bargain: Bargaining is common at flea markets and other secondhand markets in France. Be prepared to haggle with sellers to get the best price.

Be patient: Antique hunting takes time and care. Don't expect to find the perfect old right away. Be patient and keep your eyes open, and you are sure to find something special.

Here are a few of the most famous places for treasure finding in France:

> **Marché aux Puces de Saint-Ouen, Paris:**

The Marché aux Puces de Saint-Ouen is the biggest flea market in the world, and it is a great place to find antiques of all kinds.

> **Marché du Cours Saleya, Nice:**

The Marché du Cours Saleya is a flower and vegetable market, but it also has a number of shops selling antiques.

> **Brocantes:**

Brocantes are small antique markets that are held throughout France on different days of the week. You can find a list of brocantes on the website of the Comité National des Brocanteurs et Antiquaires de France.

> **Auction houses:**

There are a number of sale shops in France that sell antiques. Some of the most popular sale houses include Christie's, Sotheby's, and Drouot.

If you are looking for a truly unique antique finding experience, be sure to visit some of the smaller villages and towns in France. Many of these towns have their own secondhand shops and brocantes, and you can often find some secret gems.

Here are a few extra tips for treasure buying in France:

- **Bring cash:** Many sellers at secondhand markets and brocantes do not accept credit cards.
- **Be aware of the customs regulations:** There are some restrictions on what you can bring back into your country from France, so be sure to check the customs regulations before you travel.
- **Have fun:** Antique hunting is a great way to learn about the history and culture of France. Enjoy the experience and don't be afraid to ask questions.

With a little planning, you can have a great time antique hunting in France.

11

Language and Travel Tips

Common Phrases

Here are some popular words in French:

```
Bonjour - Hello
Bonsoir - Good evening
Au revoir - Goodbye
Merci - Thank you
S'il vous plaît - Please
Excusez-moi - Excuse me
Oui - Yes
Non - No
Je ne comprends pas - I don't understand
Parlez-vous anglais ? - Do you speak English ?
Je m'appelle ... - My name is ...
Quel est votre nom ? - What is your name ?
Où sont les toilettes ? - Where are the toilets ?
Je cherche ... - I'm looking for ...
Pouvez-vous m'aider ? - Can you help me ?
Combien ça coûte ? - How much does it cost ?
Je vais payer en espèces. - I'm going to pay in cash.
Je vais payer par carte de crédit. - I'm going to pay by
```

```
credit card.
Bon appétit - Enjoy your meal!
À votre santé - Cheers!
```

Here are some additional words that can be useful in France:

```
Je ne sais pas - I don't know
Je ne suis pas sûr - I'm not sure
Pouvez-vous répéter s'il vous plaît ? - Can you repeat that please?
Pouvez-vous parler plus lentement ? - Can you speak more slowly?
Pouvez-vous écrire cela pour moi ? - Can you write that down for me?
Je suis perdu - I'm lost
J'ai faim - I'm hungry
J'ai soif - I'm thirsty
Je suis fatigué - I'm tired
Je suis malade - I'm sick
J'ai besoin d'aide - I need help
Appelez la police - Call the police
Appelez une ambulance - Call an ambulance
```

It is always a good idea to learn a few simple words in the local language when going to a new country. This will show that you are making an effort to be respectful of the culture, and it can also be helpful in getting around and speaking with locals.

Travel Safety

France is a relatively safe place to travel to, but there are a few things you can do to stay safe and avoid any problems.

Here are some tips for trip safety in France:

Be aware of your surroundings: This is especially important in busy places, such as tourist sites and public transportation. Keep an eye on your things and be aware of people who are getting too close.

Be careful with your things: Don't leave your belongings unsupervised, especially in public places. If you are carrying a bag or backpack, keep it close to your body and don't put anything important in your back pockets.

Beware of pickpockets: Pickpocketing is a regular crime in France, especially in busy places. Be extra careful with your things in tourist sites, on public transportation, and in markets.

Be careful with your credit cards: When using your credit card, be sure to shield the PIN number from view. It is also a good idea to keep a copy of your ID and credit cards in a different place, in case they are lost or stolen.

Be aware of scams: There are a number of scams that target tourists in France. One popular scam is the "three card trick," where a group of people approach you and offer to play a card game. Another common scam is the "pigeon drop," where someone drops a big amount of money and then asks you to help them pick it up. If you are approached by someone giving you a deal that seems too good to be true, it probably is.

Be respectful of the culture: France has a rich culture and past, so it is important to be respectful of the local habits and practices. This includes dressing properly, avoiding public shows of love, and being aware of your noise level.

If you do find yourself in a situation where you feel unsafe, it is important to know what to do. Here are some tips:

- **Trust your gut:** If you feel like something is wrong, it probably is. Don't be afraid to walk away from a setting if you feel unsafe.

- **Be assertive:** If someone is approaching you or making you feel uncomfortable, don't be afraid to tell them to leave you alone.
- Get help: If you are in immediate danger, call the cops or emergency services.

By following these tips, you can help ensure a safe and fun trip to France.

Here are some extra tips for trip safety in France:

Learn a few basic French phrases: This will help you interact with people and get around more quickly.

Be prepared for medical emergencies: Pack a first-aid kit and any necessary medicines. Be sure to have a copy of your trip insurance coverage on hand.

Make copies of your important documents: This includes your passport, driver's license, credit cards, and insurance information. Leave copies of these papers at home with a trusted friend or family member.

Register with your embassy: This will help your embassy call you in case of an emergency.

By following these tips, you can help ensure a safe and fun trip to France.

Etiquette and Customs

France has a rich culture and past, and its manners and customs reflect this. It is important to be aware of these customs when visiting France, so that you can avoid any mistakes or cultural faux pas.

Greetings

- When meeting someone in France, it is normal to shake hands. If you are meeting a woman, you may also kiss her on the cheek once, on the right side.
- When meeting a group of people, start with the oldest or highest-ranking person first.
- It is polite to use the person's rank and last name when welcoming them, unless you are close friends or family.

Dining

- When eating in France, it is customary to wait until everyone at the table has been served before starting to eat.
- It is also considered nice to finish everything on your plate.
- If you are not sure which fork or spoon to use, start from the outside and work your way in.
- It is thought rude to talk with your mouth full.
- When you are finished eating, place your fork and knife together in the middle of your plate.

Other customs

- It is nice to dress properly for the event. For example, you would not want to dress too loosely for a serious event.
- It is also thought nice to be on time for visits and meetings.
- When entering someone's home, it is normal to remove your shoes.

- It is also thought rude to smoke in public places.

Here are some additional etiquette and culture tips for France:

- Avoid speaking loudly in public.
- Do not put your feet on furniture.
- Do not point at people.
- Do not talk about politics or religion with people you don't know well.
- Do not attack French society or food.
- If you are asked to someone's home for dinner, it is usual to bring a gift, such as a bottle of wine or flowers.

By following these tips, you can help ensure that you have a polite and enjoyable time in France.

Packing Essentials

Packing for a trip to France can be difficult, as you need to pack for all types of weather and activities. Here is a list of important items to pack for your trip to France, along with pictures to help you envision them:

Clothes

Comfy shoes: You'll be doing a lot of walking in France, so it's important to pack comfy shoes.

Clothes: The weather in France can be unpredictable, so it's a good idea to pack clothes so that you can adjust to the temperature.

A rain jacket or umbrella: It's always a good idea to pack a rain jacket or umbrella when going to France, as it can rain suddenly.

A scarf or shawl: A scarf or blanket can be used to keep warm or to dress up an outfit.

A dress or skirt: If you're planning on doing any fancy eating or dancing, you'll want to pack a dress or skirt.

Accessories

Sunscreen: France has a strong sun, so it's important to pack sunscreen to protect your face.

Sunglasses: Sunglasses are also important for protecting your eyes from the sun.

A hat: A hat can help keep the sun out of your eyes and protect your head from the heat.

A camera: France is a beautiful country, so you'll want to pack a camera to record all of your moments.

A power adapter: France uses a different type of power outlet than many other countries, so you'll need to pack a power adapter if you want to use your electronics.

Other essentials

Passport: Don't forget to pack your passport.

Visa: If you need a visa to enter France, be sure to ask for one in advance.

Travel insurance: Travel insurance can protect you in case of unexpected events, such as lost bags or medical problems.

Money: Be sure to exchange some cash for euros before you go to France. You can also use your credit or debit card in most places in France, but it's always a good idea to have some cash on hand.

Medicines: If you take any medicines, be sure to pack them with you. It's also a good idea to pack a copy of your prescription, in case you lose your medicine or need to get it updated while you're in France.

Optional items

- **A phrasebook:** A French phrasebook can be helpful for learning basic words and interacting with locals.
- **A travel journal:** A travel journal can be a great way to record your trip and reflect on your experiences.

Packing tips

- **Pack light:** You'll be doing a lot of walking in France, so it's important to pack light so that you're not carrying around a big bag.
- **Roll your clothes:** Rolling your clothes instead of folding them can help you save space in your bag.
- **Use packing cubes:** Packing cubes can help you organize your bags and make it easier to find what you're looking for.

- **Bring a carry-on bag:** In case your luggage is lost or delayed, it's a good idea to bring a carry-on bag with important items, such as a change of clothes, toiletries, and medicines.

By following these tips, you can pack for your trip to France and ensure that you have everything you need for a great holiday.

12

Conclusion

Further Reading and Resources

France is a country with a rich culture and past, and there are many tools available for those who want to learn more about it. Here is a list of further reading and tools in France:

- Books
- Websites

France.fr: The main website of the French Tourist Board, with information on everything from travel to culture.

France Culture: A website dedicated to French culture, with papers, talks, and movies on a range of themes.

RFI: The website of Radio France Internationale, a French public radio station that plays in over 30 languages.

Le Monde: The website of Le Monde, a French daily newspaper.

Libération: The website of Libération, another French daily newspaper.

- Museums

Musée du Louvre: One of the largest and most famous museums in the world, with a collection that spans thousands of years of art and history.

Musée d'Orsay: A museum dedicated to Impressionist and Post-Impressionist art.

Centre Pompidou: A museum of modern and contemporary art.

Musée Rodin: A museum dedicated to the work of Auguste Rodin.

Musée Picasso: A museum dedicated to the work of Pablo Picasso.

- Language schools

Alliance Française: A world network of language schools that offer French lessons for all levels.

Institut Français: A French cultural group that offers French lessons and other cultural events.

Berlitz: A language school that offers French lessons in over 70 countries.

Inlingua: A language school that offers French lessons in over 30 countries.

Wall Street English: A language school that offers French lessons in over 25 countries.

These are just a few of the many tools available for those who want to learn more about France. With its rich culture and past, France has something to offer everyone.

Feedback and Contact Information

French people are generally polite and quiet, but they do value comments. If you have any feedback, whether it's positive or negative, it's best to give it in a helpful and polite way.

Here are a few tips for giving comments in France:

- Be straight and to the point: French folks value open communication.
- Be detailed and provide examples: This will help the person understand your comments and how they can improve.
- Be positive and offer ideas: Don't just attack, offer answers.
- Be respectful: Even if you have bad comments, be polite and professional.

Contact Information in France

Here are some useful contact information in France:

```
Emergency number: 112
Police: 17
Fire department: 18
Ambulance: 15
English-speaking helpline: 116 117
```

```
Tourist information: 08 92 68 30 60
```

You can also find contact information for government organizations, companies, and people on the French government website: https://www.service-public.fr/

Here are some additional tips for giving feedback and getting contact information in France:

- If you're giving comments to a business or group, you can usually find their contact information on their website or social media pages.
- If you're giving feedback to a government organization, you can find their contact information on the French government website.
- If you're having trouble finding contact information, you can try looking for the company or organization's name on Google Maps.
- If you're still having trouble finding contact information, you can try calling the English-speaking helpline at 116 117.

CONCLUSION

Final Note

We are delighted that you picked the "France Travel Guide 2024" to travel with while you explore France World. We hope that reading this book has motivated you and given you important information for your next trip.

If you want to add to your library of helpful travel books and learn about new desirable holiday places, go to our author's page on Amazon.

Remember that finding new places is a constant process that opens our eyes and hearts to the wonders and variety of the world.

Travel happily, absorb yourself in other cultures, and make life-changing moments.

Have a safe trip, and may your trips be full of surprises, thrills, and important contacts.

- Melisa's Travel Guides

Printed in Great Britain
by Amazon